PLEASING
YOU
IS DESTROYING
ME

PLEASING YOU IS DESTROYING ME

Bobbie Reed, Ph.D.

WORD PUBLISHING

Dallas · London · Vancouver · Melbourne

Pleasing You Is Destroying Me
Copyright ©1992 by Bobbie Reed

Unless otherwise indicated, Scripture quotations are from
the King James Version of the Bible (KJV).

Library of Congress Cataloging-in-Publication Data

Reed, Bobbie.
  Pleasing you is destroying me: how to stop being controlled
by your people-pleasing habits / Bobbie Reed.
    p. cm.
  ISBN 0–8499–3347–1 (trade paper) :
  1. Assertiveness (Psychology)—Religious aspects—Chris-
tianity. 2. Assertiveness training. 3. Christian life—1960-
I. Title
BV4647.A78R44 1992
158' .2—dc20   92–8367
                                                 CIP

Printed in the United States of America

2 3 4 5 9 LB 9 8 7 6 5 4 3 2 1

To Steve Hensley,
whose gentle, caring confrontation
caused me to face the people pleaser I was,
and whose wise counsel showed me how to change

Contents

Acknowledgments

I want to thank the many people who took time out of their busy schedules to share with me their stories of people-pleasing behaviors. All of the stories in this book are true, although some of the names have been changed and circumstances slightly altered to protect confidentiality.

I would also like to thank my husband, Ed, for his valuable feedback and assistance with this project.

Introduction

There was a box somewhere in the closet, one left over from Christmas. Yes. There in the corner of the top shelf. With just a little tissue paper, the velvet robe filled the box in perfectly. You could just make out the maroon through the tissue.

I like it, I thought to myself as I placed the box with the other things I'd be taking to work that morning.

It had taken all night and I was exhausted, but I had finally finished it. The thrill of having completed my task and having it turn out so beautifully gave me the extra boost of energy I needed to pack the kids' lunches and get ready for work.

Every bone in my body ached, but I was eagerly anticipating Barbara's pleasure as she fingered the beautiful robe, imagining her praise of my work and her gratitude for my sacrifice to finish the robe for her in such a hurry.

I did a great job, I thought as I remembered how Barbara had briefly visited my desk yesterday just before five to ask how the robe was coming. (What a presumption that was!) "Bobbie, I'm going on vacation after work tomorrow, and I just *have* to have that robe to take along. Can you bring it tomorrow morning?" Well, nothing like a little urgency to stoke the creative fires. . . .

I caught myself smiling into the rearview mirror all the way to work. *Everybody's going to gush over this one*, I thought. Stifling a yawn, I carried the package to Barbara's office. Only the light wasn't on. Sticking my head in the door, I saw a cleared desk, nothing more.

I asked a co-worker, "Has anyone seen Barbara this morning?"

"Barbara left on her vacation last night. She won't be back for a week," said Stacy.

Stunned and angry, I walked slowly back to my office. Suddenly, I felt the fatigue that my adrenalin had masked all morning. I had stayed up *all night* to work on this stupid robe!

When Barbara returned from her vacation she accepted the robe for which I had sacrificed my time and schedule. All she said was, "Thanks." I was angry—with Barbara, with the robe, and with myself. All I did, though, was smile and return to my desk.

Being a people pleaser hurts. And I am a people pleaser. At least I was until I saw how detrimental—even destructive—it was to my own well-being. It took the honesty of a friend named Steve—and a lot of hard work—for me to kick the people-pleasing habit. And if I could do it, so can you.

WHAT IS A PEOPLE PLEASER?

Don't misunderstand me. The desire to please others and to obtain approval is a natural one. Actually, one of our deepest needs is to love and be loved. We need approval and acceptance from others. Therefore, in an effort to escape rejection, we strive to behave in ways that ensure that we will be accepted.

This is not necessarily wrong. If we want to live together peaceably, we must take into consideration the needs and desires of others and learn to cooperate. We teach our children to obey the rules and to behave in socially acceptable ways. We also allow them to experience the consequences of their choices—both positive and negative (including punishment, loss, or rejection)—so they may learn the value of living within certain broad guidelines.

There is nothing wrong with choosing to be pleasant, accommodating, and courteous. If we did not make such choices, we would find ourselves in a hostile, selfish world where every difference of opinion would become a major battle. So for society as a whole, we accept good manners as a means of order, dictating certain pleasing behaviors, such as "Guests get to choose," "Ladies first," and "Don't make a scene in public." We learn to be polite, to say "please" and "thank you," to ask instead of demand.

We sometimes choose to put another's desires ahead of our own. For example, as a way of showing love, we will watch a movie thriller with a friend when we are really in the mood for a comedy.

When considering whether to insist on doing things our way or doing them someone else's way, we take into consideration the ramifications of our choices. There are times when we will choose to please others just as there were times when Jesus chose to please others, such as when He went to the cross for us (Rom. 15:1–3; Luke 22:39–42).

Pleasing others becomes a problem when people crave the approval of others to the extent that they are incapable of independent choice. *A people pleaser is someone who is "happy" only when actively working at earning the approval of others at any cost, including self-betrayal.*

Of course we all want approval. It feels good when someone gives us a nod of agreement, and a compliment can virtually make our day. People pleasers, on the other hand, have an *overdeveloped* need for approval, which creates problems for them and the people with whom they come in contact. People pleasers live in constant fear of rejection. Yet no matter how hard they try to please everyone, someone will be displeased.

People pleasers perceive any of this negative feedback as personal rejection and are usually left devastated. To avoid this, they will often hold back their opinions or ideas so they won't be considered bossy, demanding, controlling, unreasonable, or wrong. This pattern usually makes people pleasers passive observers of life rather than active participants who make choices for themselves. They are vulnerable to exploitation by people who aren't as concerned about pleasing others, and their personal growth is often blocked because too much of themselves is negotiable (beliefs, priorities, ambitions, desires, preferences, and opinions).

People pleasers are addicted to approval and will do almost anything to gain it. If approval is out of the question, they will settle for acceptance or just attention.

People pleasers generally have a low self-esteem in that they do not consider themselves worthy of being pleased. Adults who have grown up with a desperate need for approval have usually failed to develop either a healthy sense of who they are or a strong sense of self-worth. They have an idea that they probably deserve respect, but they are unable to stand up, speak out, or reach for the love and affection they want so desperately.

People pleasers don't believe they will be accepted by others unless they are actively working at winning approval, so they go to extraordinary lengths to win applause. They dress to please. They act to please. They say what they think others want to hear—or they keep their mouths shut except to compliment others. They spend their hard-earned money on gifts for others. They give more of their time and energy than they can afford to give. They are great self-sacrificers. They live as performers rather than as themselves. By doing and investing everything they have to earn the applause of others, they relinquish control of their lives. People pleasers secretly believe that they don't measure up by "being," so they make up for their perceived shortcomings by "doing."

People pleasers work twice as hard as other people in their relationships. They are usually prompt (not wanting to keep anyone else waiting), gentle listeners (not venturing to express a conflicting opinion), and eager servants ("Please, let *me* do that!"). People pleasers are not pushy except when smothering others with gifts, favors, and helpfulness. They go along with what everyone else wants to do and rarely make suggestions. This makes people pleasers nice to have around—you can have things your way and have lots of help for whatever projects you are doing.

Sometimes, however, people pleasers get tired of being taken for granted, of not being thought of as having valid opinions or ideas, and of giving in.

Then, too, it can be quite wearisome to be around someone who is forever apologizing, kowtowing, and deferring. So, the very things people pleasers do to gain approval often have the opposite effect, and the persons people pleasers have tried to win over grow weary of having them around and end up rejecting them.

The secret of making healthy choices, in terms of pleasing others, comes in finding and maintaining a proper balance. We must please others sometimes. We must please ourselves sometimes. On the continuum of choices, we can find five basic positions:

ME	*PLEASING*	*YOU*
Me Only   Me First   We   You First   You Only

Pleasing Continuum

Me Only. At the extreme end of the pleasing continuum are people who please only themselves, all of the time, and at the expense of others. They demand their own ways and will fight to the bitter end if opposed. They often try to choose for others because they are convinced that they know what is best not only for themselves, but also for everyone else. These people are highly critical, yet seemingly oblivious to the criticism of others.

Me First. In the next position on this scale are people who please themselves first and then, if it doesn't inconvenience them, take into consideration the needs and desires of others. These people don't get their own way so much by demanding as they do by manipulating, persuading, and persisting. They are a bit more gentle than the *Me Only* people, but they are still not the people you think of asking first when you need a favor.

We. *We* people have found the proper balance between asking and giving. They are aware of and take care of their own needs and desires, but they also weigh carefully the needs and wants of others. In the process they usually find ways to accommodate both. *We* people take responsibility for their ideas, opinions, and needs and don't depend on others for a sense of worthiness. They have a strong sense of self-esteem and a caring attitude toward others. In relationships, *We* people feel valued, they value others, and they are affirming.

You First. Some people almost always defer to the needs and wishes of others, pleasing themselves only as an afterthought or when there is no one else around to please. However, when they make independent choices they need frequent feedback from others about the validity of their choices and decisions. If someone thinks his decision was wrong, a *You First* person will reevaluate it. *You First* people are people pleasers most of the time, and their self-esteem is tentative at best.

You Only. Extreme people pleasers are happy only when they are working to please others. They lack a well-developed sense of their own needs and desires because they are so accustomed to giving in to others. They have no expectations of their own. If there isn't someone around to please, they look for someone to help, assist, and give to. *You Only* people have lost the "I" in their relationships.

Some of these descriptions may fit you while others do not. Perhaps you tend to be a people pleaser but do not give in to those tendencies most of the time. Take the self-tests at the end of this section to see where you fit on the pleasing continuum.

Some people pleasers never break out of the pattern. They seek to please everyone all of the time. Others have learned to be *We* people in some relationships, but not others. They might be *We* people with co-workers and friends, but people pleasers in romantic relationships. Still others can be assertive and confident in dating relationships and with friends, but at work they are insecure and frequently exhibit people-pleasing behaviors.

While most of us would agree that we behave like people pleasers in some instances, we don't want to admit that we subscribe to the beliefs behind those behaviors. Whether by behavior or belief or both, if you usually find yourself giving in to others, it's likely that you are doing so because you have some level of fear of being yourself, trusting the relationship, or creating a situation in which you might be rejected. In other words, if you often agree to do things you don't want to do, if you feel that people take advantage of your good nature, if you sacrifice what you want to do most of the time, or if you wonder if you're appreciated for all those wonderful things you do for your family and friends, you're a people pleaser.

People pleasers are afraid to be themselves. This book is about getting over that fear. It is a road map for people pleasers who want to learn to move to the *We* position on the pleasing continuum. If you are sometimes (or always) a people pleaser, this book is for you. It will challenge you to stand up, speak up, and reach out for what you want, to be yourself. It will encourage you to stop searching for approval and waiting for applause from others and to listen to your inner voice and seek confirmation from within and from God. It will help you find the person God would have you become— a channel of His love for others and a giver rather than a needy person.

The skills presented here are those needed for making a successful journey from people pleasing to living free. Paul said in Gal. 1:10 that we must choose to please God, not people. People will disappoint us and let us down. God won't. He's waiting for us to discover ourselves as He created us to be. He's given each of us spiritual gifts and natural abilities. Some of us have failed even to open these gifts to see what He has given us. How sad to think that some people will only recognize these marvelous gifts when they get to heaven—gifts they never used.

I challenge you to start today. Unwrap your gifts. Unleash your potential. Discover who you are and how successful and abundant your life can become!

Self-Tests
Are You a People Pleaser?

Three different self-assessments are provided below to help you evaluate the degree to which you are or are not a people pleaser in three different areas of your life: at work, with friends, and with a spouse or romantic partner. The self-assessments can be taken singly or all at one time. There is a scoring chart for each self-assessment, and a comparison chart for you to use to compare the ways you are similar or different in these three different roles/relationships.

Most people have some tendencies toward people pleasing, and most of us sometimes choose to please ourselves first. There are not necessarily "wrong" responses. Try to be as honest as you can with evaluating how you would respond to the different situations.

Five different completions are given for each of the sentences given in the self-assessments. Mark each completion with a number from 1 to 5, with 1 being least like you and 5 being most like you. Be sure to give each completion a number, even if you don't feel that any of the responses are exactly those you would choose.

Self-Assessment #1
How Are You at Work?

1. If I believed my boss were being very unfair to me, I would tell myself . . .

   ___ a. He/she is the boss, and I must accept his/her decision.

   ___ b. It is my fault, I must be doing something wrong.

   ___ c. The boss is wrong and ought to be straightened out.

   ___ d. The boss doesn't know what he/she is doing and needs to listen to me.

   ___ e. To think through what I want to say to the boss, schedule an appointment and discuss it with him/her.

2. In a meeting at work, if I have a dissenting opinion from the rest of the group, I tell myself . . .

   ___ a. I am right and the rest of the group is wrong. I have a responsibility to speak out.

   ___ b. The group wouldn't listen to me if I did speak up.

   ___ c. I don't want to start an argument, so I ought to just keep quiet.

   ___ d. I will listen to everyone else, evaluate their ideas, introduce my idea and objectively discuss the pros and cons of all ideas.

   ___ e. I am right, and I can probably convince the others if I speak up.

3. If I want something from my boss (e.g., a change of assignment, a raise, or new office furniture), I tell myself . . .

    ___ a. I really shouldn't ask because it might make the boss angry.

    ___ b. I might have a chance at getting what I want if I submit a written request complete with justification and a full recital of the benefits to the company.

    ___ c. The boss owes me and ought to give me what I want.

    ___ d. I need to watch for when the boss is in a good mood and then hint about (or teasingly ask for) what I want.

    ___ e. I ought to quit if I don't get what I want.

4. At work, I tell myself . . .

    ___ a. I need to help out as many people as I can.

    ___ b. I like to be considered helpful.

    ___ c. I only need to do my own job, not everyone else's.

    ___ d. I don't mind doing extra work as long as everyone else pitches in also.

    ___ e. I am not paid to take on extra work.

5. When my boss compliments me, I tell myself . . .

    ___ a. I'm on his/her good side now.

    ___ b. He/she didn't see all that I didn't do right.

    ___ c. Next time I'll try to do a better job.

    ___ d. It's about time he/she noticed how hard I work.

    ___ e. It's nice to be appreciated.

6. The criticism I most hate to hear at work is . . .

    ___ a. You are indecisive.

    ___ b. You don't do enough work.

    ___ c. You don't have the proper perspective.

    ___ d. You aren't always nice to people.

    ___ e. You are a pushover.

7. When it is time for lunch or a break at work, I . . .

    ___ a. Welcome a chance to relax and visit with co-workers.

    ___ b. Feel guilty if I take breaks and usually continue working while I eat my lunch.

    ___ c. Hate it when people interrupt my lunch or break with work-related questions.

    ___ d. Feel that I can't take a break unless my work is all caught up.

    ___ e. Tell myself that I work hard and deserve a break.

8. As an employee, I tell myself that . . .

    ___ a. I am a conscientious and qualified employee.

    ___ b. I am inadequate in some areas and must work extra hard to make up for these.

    ___ c. I am stupid when I make a mistake, and then I worry about what will happen if someone finds out.

    ___ d. I am the best and most qualified employee.

    ___ e. I have a lot of strengths and am working on correcting my weaknesses.

9. At work, when someone has a problem I . . .

    ___ a. Want to help if I can, so I usually get involved by offering suggestions.

    ___ b. Don't mind giving advice, if I am consulted.

    ___ c. Hate to see people hurting, so I feel responsible for helping them solve their problems.

___ d. Listen to people's problems and ask them what they are planning to do to solve their problems.

___ e. Tell myself it is not my problem, and don't get involved.

10. If there is someone I admire at work but with whom I have never become acquainted, I tell myself . . .

___ a. We are equals; I could contact that person and suggest we have coffee break together and get acquainted.

___ b. I'm just as good as he/she is, and he/she would be lucky to meet me.

___ c. I am probably smarter/more qualified than that person.

___ d. He/she probably wouldn't like to get to know me.

___ e. I wouldn't want to bother him/her so I shouldn't try to get acquainted.

Score Sheet
Relationships at Work

Transfer your numbers from the previous pages to the appropriate spaces on the score sheet. Add each column.

	Me Only	Me First	We	You First	You Only
1. Confronting	1c _____	1d _____	1e _____	1a _____	1b _____
2. Expressing opinions	2a _____	2e _____	2d _____	2c _____	2b _____
3. Expressing wants	3e _____	3c _____	3b _____	3d _____	3a _____
4. Taking on tasks	4e _____	4c _____	4d _____	4b _____	4a _____
5. Getting compliments	5d _____	5a _____	5e _____	5b _____	5c _____
6. Taking criticism	6e _____	6a _____	6c _____	6d _____	6b _____
7. Using leisure time	7c _____	7e _____	7a _____	7d _____	7b _____
8. Self-esteem	8d _____	8a _____	8e _____	8c _____	8b _____
9. Fixing the world	9e _____	9b _____	9d _____	9a _____	9c _____
10. Initiating contact	10c _____	10b _____	10a _____	10e _____	10d _____
TOTALS	_____	_____	_____	_____	_____

Self-Assessment #2
How Are You with Friends?

1. When a friend disappoints me, I tell myself . . .
   ___ a. If I want to keep the friendship, I must hide my disappointment and go out of my way to be nice to this person so he/she will want to treat me better.
   ___ b. I must have let my friend down in some way, so it is probably my fault.
   ___ c. I can't trust him/her, so I won't depend upon that friend again.
   ___ d. I need to meet with my friend and honestly share my hurt so we can resolve the problem.
   ___ e. He/she isn't a very good friend, so I should be careful in the friendship.

2. If I am with several friends and I disagree with the general direction of the discussion, I tell myself . . .
   ___ a. It's okay to express my opinions along with the others.
   ___ b. I need to try to convince the others they are wrong.
   ___ c. I need to keep quiet so no one will know I disagree and I don't start a big discussion.
   ___ d. I prefer to refrain from participating in the discussion rather than express disagreement.
   ___ e. I am right and have a responsibility to let others know the truth.

3. If I want a big favor from a friend, I feel . . .
  ____ a. Comfortable in asking for what I want.
  ____ b. Confident in asking for what I want.
  ____ c. Entitled to ask for what I want.
  ____ d. Hesitant to ask for what I want.
  ____ e. Afraid of asking for what I want.

4. When we get together as a group to do something such as give a party, hold a potluck, or organize a community project, I tell myself . . .
  ____ a. Everyone will share in the planning and the implementation.
  ____ b. I don't need to do anything; let the others take care of things.
  ____ c. I enjoy helping and don't mind doing more than my share of the work.
  ____ d. People want me included because I work hard and get things done.
  ____ e. I need to let people know how I think things should be organized and then let them do it.

5. When a friend compliments my appearance, I feel . . .
  ____ a. Embarrassed and as if I ought to compliment him/her in return.
  ____ b. Comfortable saying "Thank you."
  ____ c. Grateful to be noticed.
  ____ d. Indifferent because I know how I look.
  ____ e. Entitled to the compliment.

6. When my friends criticize me, I feel . . .
  ____ a. Depressed and consider making changes.
  ____ b. Insulted by the criticism.
  ____ c. Crushed and work to regain approval.
  ____ d. Willing to make changes if they are necessary.
  ____ e. Indifferent to the criticism.

7. When my friends and I get together for leisure time
activities, I tell myself . . .
    ___ a. Work some, relax some.
    ___ b. Relax and enjoy the event.
    ___ c. Help with tasks if asked.
    ___ d. See what you can do to help everyone
            have a good time.
    ___ e. Don't relax until all of the tasks are done
            and everyone else is having a good time.

8. When I'm with my friends, I feel . . .
    ___ a. I am superior in many ways.
    ___ b. Grateful when they include me.
    ___ c. No need to compare myself with them,
            because I feel comfortable with myself.
    ___ d. Somewhat superior to some of them.
    ___ e. Out of place; I wish I were smarter, more
            knowledgeable, or had achieved more.

9. When one of my friends has a problem, I feel . . .
    ___ a. Responsible for finding a way to help
            him/her solve the problem.
    ___ b. Unhappy until the problem is solved.
    ___ c. Willing to listen and to help if asked.
    ___ d. No responsibility for getting involved.
    ___ e. Irritated that the friend hasn't resolved
            the problem, especially when the prob-
            lem is affecting our friendship or my life.

10. If there is someone in a social setting I think I would
like to meet, I tell myself . . .
    ___ a. I'm just as good as he/she is, and he/she
            would be happy to meet me.
    ___ b. He/she probably wouldn't like to get to
            know me.
    ___ c. I am probably smarter/more fun than
            that person.

___ d. I wouldn't want to bother him/her, so I shouldn't try to get acquainted.

___ e. We are equals and I could contact that person and suggest that we get together and get acquainted.

Score Sheet
Relationships with Friends

Transfer your numbers from the previous pages to the appropriate spaces on the score sheet. Add each column.

	Me Only	Me First	We	You First	You Only
1. Confronting	1c _____	1e _____	1d _____	1b _____	1a _____
2. Expressing opinions	2e _____	2b _____	2a _____	2d _____	2c _____
3. Expressing wants	3c _____	3a _____	3b _____	3d _____	3e _____
4. Taking on tasks	4b _____	4e _____	4a _____	4c _____	4d _____
5. Getting compliments	5d _____	5e _____	5b _____	5a _____	5c _____
6. Taking criticism	6b _____	6e _____	6d _____	6a _____	6c _____
7. Using leisure time	7b _____	7c _____	7a _____	7e _____	7d _____
8. Self-esteem	8a _____	8d _____	8c _____	8e _____	8b _____
9. Fixing the world	9e _____	9d _____	9c _____	9b _____	9a _____
10. Initiating contact	10c _____	10a _____	10e _____	10d _____	10b _____
TOTALS	_____	_____	_____	_____	_____

Self-Assessment #3
How Are You with Your Spouse/Romantic Partner?

1. If my spouse/romantic partner has a habit which is annoying to me, I tell myself . . .
    ___ a. It is in the best interest of the relationship to talk to him/her lovingly about the habit and ask if he/she would consider changing that habit.
    ___ b. Not to say anything because he/she might leave me if I do—and nothing is worth that.
    ___ c. I have to tell him/her to stop the habit.
    ___ d. He/she must stop.
    ___ e. I don't want to hurt his/her feelings by saying anything.

2. When my spouse/romantic partner and I disagree about a subject, I feel . . .
    ___ a. Angry that my partner won't acknowledge that I am right.
    ___ b. Irritated by the disagreement.
    ___ c. Willing to listen to his/her side, share my opinion and discuss both points of view.
    ___ d. Concerned that the argument might damage our relationship, so I usually give in.
    ___ e. Afraid of losing the relationship, so I won't voice my opinion in the first place.

3. If I want my spouse/romantic partner to do something for me, I feel . . .
    ___ a. Confident about asking for what I want.

    ___ b. Comfortable asking him/her for what I want.

    ___ c. Hesitant about asking for what I want.

    ___ d. Afraid of asking for what I want.

    ___ e. Entitled to ask and receive what I want.

4. At home (mine, his/hers, or ours) with my spouse/ romantic partner, I tell myself . . .

    ___ a. We share the household chores pretty equally.

    ___ b. He/she enjoys waiting on me.

    ___ c. I enjoy waiting on him/her.

    ___ d. I wish I could be waited on, but I end up doing most of the work anyway.

    ___ e. I am willing to help if I need to.

5. If my spouse/romantic partner compliments me, I feel . . .

    ___ a. Entitled to the compliment.

    ___ b. Embarrassed by the compliment.

    ___ c. Grateful for the compliment.

    ___ d. Pleased with myself.

    ___ e. Comfortable saying "Thank you."

6. If my spouse/romantic partner criticizes me, I feel . . .

    ___ a. Crushed and afraid of losing the relationship, so I work to regain approval.

    ___ b. Willing to look at the criticism to see if it is valid and try to change if warranted.

    ___ c. Insulted by the criticism.

    ___ d. Indifferent to the criticism.

    ___ e. Depressed and consider making changes.

7. If my spouse/romantic partner and I take a trip or plan an activity together, I tell myself . . .

    ___ a. We will split the planning and the chores and enjoy the trip/activity.

___ b. Let the other person take the responsi-
        bility for the planning and preparations.
___ c. I enjoy serving the other person, and so
        I will do as much as I can of the plan-
        ning and preparations, even more than
        my share.
___ d. I am willing to help if I am needed.
___ e. I will enjoy myself as soon as I get every-
        thing done.

8. When I am alone with my spouse/romantic partner,
I feel . . .
___ a. Envious of his/her strengths.
___ b. Confident and secure in our relationship.
___ c. Desirous of being what he/she wants me
        to be.
___ d. Very good about myself because of my
        achievements and accomplishments.
___ e. Aware of being superior.

9. If my spouse/romantic partner has a problem outside of our relationship, I feel . . .
___ a. Willing to listen to his/her problem and
        ask what he/she plans to do about it.
___ b. Responsible for "fixing" things and mak-
        ing his/her world go right.
___ c. It is not my concern.
___ d. Desirous of helping him/her solve the
        problem.
___ e. Interested, but not involved.

10. If I really want the evening to be more romantic
than it is so far, I feel . . .
___ a. No hesitation in becoming physically de-
        manding in spite of my spouse/romantic
        partner's mood.
___ b. Afraid of voicing my feelings, so I try to

determine my partner's mood and go along with that.

___ c. Hesitant about making the first move, so I drop hints about what I'd like to have happen.

___ d. Comfortable becoming physically affectionate and initiating contact.

___ e. It is okay to become persistently seductive.

Score Sheet
Relationship with
My Romantic Partner

Transfer your numbers from the previous pages to the appropriate spaces on the score sheet. Add each column.

	Me Only	Me First	We	You First	You Only
1. Confronting	1d _____	1c _____	1a _____	1e _____	1b _____
2. Expressing opinions	2a _____	2b _____	2c _____	2d _____	2e _____
3. Expressing wants	3e _____	3a _____	3b _____	3c _____	3d _____
4. Taking on tasks	4b _____	4e _____	4a _____	4c _____	4d _____
5. Getting compliments	5a _____	5d _____	5e _____	5b _____	5c _____
6. Taking criticism	6c _____	6d _____	6b _____	6e _____	6a _____
7. Using leisure time	7b _____	7d _____	7a _____	7e _____	7c _____
8. Self-esteem	8e _____	8b _____	8d _____	8a _____	8c _____
9. Fixing the world	9c _____	9e _____	9a _____	9d _____	9b _____
10. Initiating contact	10a _____	10e _____	10d _____	10c _____	10b _____
TOTALS	_____	_____	_____	_____	_____

Comparison Totals

	Me Only	Me First	We	You First	You Only
Relationships:					
At Work	_____	_____	_____	_____	_____
With Friends	_____	_____	_____	_____	_____
With Partner	_____	_____	_____	_____	_____
TOTALS	_____	_____	_____	_____	_____

A score of 40–50 indicates a strong tendency toward a position; 20–39 indicates a moderate tendency toward a position; 10–19 indicates very little tendency toward a position.

Part I

*Take Stock—
Become More
Open*

1

Examine Your Lifestyle

I've known Edna for several years. She is forty-seven. Each morning she dresses carefully, coordinating her outfit from selections recommended by a salesclerk who had insisted that browns and greens were "her colors." Edna doesn't really like the browns and greens of her wardrobe, but she had not been able to say no and ended up buying everything the salesclerk suggested. Each day Edna goes to a job she considers boring. But she has never applied for a promotion or transfer, even though she has been at her current level and position for the last seven years. Why? About once a month her boss tells her that she was "made for this job" and that he "couldn't live" without her. This makes Edna feel good and important and needed. She likes that feeling.

Edna never sends food back in a restaurant, preferring to eat ill-prepared food or just leave it on her plate. She even has difficulty returning defective merchandise.

Edna spends most of her time working hard to please other people and has problems saying no to the requests of others. As a result, she has no time for herself. She anxiously tries to fit into the molds others have shaped for her, and she tries to be the person she thinks others want her to be. All her energy is drained, and she is constantly tired. Because she doesn't use common sense in evaluating the expectations of others—she simply tries to comply—she has become a nobody to herself and to others. Edna is an extreme people pleaser.

Because Edna strives so hard to please everybody, including strangers, she has a strong sense that others ought to please her, as well. After all, that would be only fair. Unfortunately, other people do not live up to Edna's expectations. Any compliments, gifts, surprises, and favors done for Edna are never enough. She is always needy, always empty, always wanting to be refilled with approval from others.

> *What about you? Are you like Edna in some ways? Do you have trouble saying no? Do you always do what others ask of you without complaining?*

THE MAKING OF A PEOPLE PLEASER

What causes a person to develop a people-pleasing lifestyle? There are several possibilities.

1. *We learn it.* Early in life we learn that the quickest way to get approval is to do what other people

want us to do. We also learn that the quickest way to lose that approval is to disagree or to fail to live up to the expectations of others. Some parents teach their children that they must conform in order to be loved. Some parents are constantly critical; others see their roles as "drill sergeants." Absentee parents and parents who are either constantly rejecting or abusive, or even constantly passive, can contribute. Children in such families grow up believing they are worthy only when they are obedient.

In most families young children are told what to think, what to choose, and what to do since they are not yet mature enough to make their own decisions. Good children are expected to go along with what they are told. Obedience is rewarded; disobedience is punished. To place the burden of choice on children who cannot yet reason or decide wisely is foolish, and parents rightly make such decisions for their children.

As children mature they are given increasingly more responsibility, learning as they grow up to make wise and thoughtful decisions. Unfortunately, some parents never allow their children to progress to the point where they learn to make their own choices. These children are not able to assert themselves, express their own opinions, develop their own personalities, or take those first steps toward independence and maturity. Instead, their parents expect total compliance without question. *Children raised in these families learn to obey to survive.*

My own people-pleasing tendencies began when I was a child. I remember going with my folks to visit their friends. I would quietly sit alone all evening on the couch because my daddy wanted me to behave. I remember my chubby little legs didn't quite reach the floor. I would listen to the adults talking and look longingly toward the other children having fun romping around and making noise. I wanted to have fun, too, but I wanted to please my daddy more. Sitting there quietly became my survival technique.

As children grow up they form friendships outside of the home. If they do not receive acceptance at home, they seek approval from their peers. Dress, speech, and other preferences are copied from the group, because being different means being mocked, criticized, or even rejected. *Children learn to conform to belong.*

As I was growing up, I never received the approval I felt I needed from my parents. So I decided to settle for the approval of my friends. To earn that approval, I became the most daring person they ever saw! I would do anything they dared me to do, never letting them see how frightened I was. When I really wanted to impress them, I would stand in the middle of the street and stare calmly at the cars racing straight at me. Although my heart was pounding furiously, I never moved. The cars would have to swerve to miss me. My friends were amazed—and impressed. But they didn't seem to like me any better. When I got in trouble (a friend of my parents happened to be in one of the cars that had to take evasive action to avoid hitting me) one of my "friends" told me that my stunt was dumb. So much for peer approval. *Children learn to "buy" approval by being daredevils or class clowns, or by giving others presents or money.*

As children grow into young adults they learn that pleasing a "significant other" is a great way to show love and to receive love in return. As long as the partners are pleasing one another, the relationship continues. *People pleasers learn to give and to do in order to be loved.*

Young adulthood, in the late teens and early twenties, is a stage of development described by Gail Sheehy in *Passages* as "pulling up the roots." During this time most young people attempt to move toward self-definition and identity. They begin to experiment with being different. If they receive encouragement and support from family and friends, they will learn to stand up for what they want, believe, and consider important. Their self-concepts are strengthened. As they gain experience with being different and still being accepted, they increase their courage to continue their personal development. Decisions are made about what career to pursue. Personal preferences are acknowledged, even if they are not in sync with those of the rest of the peer group. Independence becomes more important than being cared for, and the need to belong becomes more selective.

This is not the case with people pleasers. Although some will ultimately decide that it is important to meet their own needs, most children who have grown up as people pleasers continue to be people pleasers in order to assure that acceptance and love they so desperately need from others.

In some ways, Edna, at forty-seven, is still about twenty years old emotionally. She is unable to handle any conflict with her parents or other authority figures because she internalizes any conflict as rebellion on her part. And Edna knows from her growing-up years that rebellion is unacceptable and will result in a withdrawal of approval. Outwardly, Edna performs well enough in life and on the job, but she is still fulfilling roles she perceives have been chosen for her.

People like Edna, who have never broken away from the need for approval from others or who have never formed a strong definition of self, often develop a people-pleasing lifestyle. They are still trying to live up to the "truisms" they have heard all of their lives, like "Father knows best." People pleasers will even do things they don't want to do or don't believe in because an authority figure (parental or otherwise) wants them to.

2. *We get stuck.* Other people pleasers do not progress through the breaking-away stage because they

have unresolved relationships in their past. My friend
Shelley, for example, cannot remember ever receiving
a compliment from her mother. No matter how good
her grades were, no matter how well-behaved she was,
Shelley never heard words of approval from her mother.
She remembers worrying, even as a small child, that if
she weren't good enough her mother would leave home,
as did the mother of one of her friends. So Shelley kept
her room clean, her toys put away, and her bed made.
She made good grades in school. She was quiet and well-
mannered, but inside she was always fearful. Whenever
her mother would get angry at her for some small
problem, Shelley would get physically ill.

Shelley grew up trying to earn approval from
any woman in authority (teacher, boss, leader) to make
up for the perceived lack of maternal approval as she
was growing up. Today Shelley is pleasant and courteous to others, but she still has not made the
transition to assertively taking responsibility for her
own life.

3. *We react.* Still other people become people
pleasers as a result of a traumatic experience. In Rex's
case, the move to people-pleasing behaviors came later
in life. Rex had always been a bit of a reckless adven-
turer. He was the first to try anything as a child, and
as an adult he was not afraid to go out on a limb. He
was assertive and not threatened by conflict. Rex was
married at twenty-five and had what he thought was
a terrific marriage. He was shocked and devastated
when his wife of ten years left him for another man.
Rex shut down emotionally, vowing never to be hurt
again. His self-esteem suffered as he began to question everything he was and everything he did. Rex
began to look to other people for direction and
affirmation. He became tentative about voicing opinions, shy of conflict, and needy for approval. Rex
became a people pleaser as an adult.

There are many other possible scenarios. The result, however, is the same: a people-pleasing lifestyle.

What about you? Did you learn to be a people pleaser as a child? Did your parents impress upon you the need to obey to be valued?

Some people find that as they grow older, mature more, and settle into a comfortable personal identity, they begin to choose to please others more than they did before. Perhaps they no longer feel they must struggle to carve out a niche or earn respect. Perhaps they fear that they will be discounted because they are older than the bright, young yuppies who often hold center-stage in the corporate world. Perhaps there is simply a need to be more giving than taking.

The bottom line is that choosing to please others is okay as long as it is a conscious choice. Feeling as if one *must* please others is an unhealthy relinquishing of one's freedom of choice—and this is wrong for all of us.

DANGERS OF BEING A PEOPLE PLEASER

Although people on the receiving end of a people pleaser's endless giving may find it quite enjoyable for a while, it can be and usually is destructive for the people pleasers. In fact, there are several dangers inherent in developing a people-pleasing lifestyle.

1. You may become a victim. Other people soon come to take advantage of the people pleaser's willingness to always be the one to give in. Edna's boss knows that he can always ask Edna to stay late or make the unpopular mail run. Other employees tend to argue that it isn't their turn, and Edna's boss finds that it's usually easier to just ask Edna since she'll always say yes and won't argue.

2. *You may become a rescuer.* People pleasers tend to take on the problems of others and try to make their worlds go right. When Shelley heard that a friend had trouble with a car, she went out and shopped for another car for that person, arranging for the best deal and then let the friend know how the car could be obtained. As in this case, Shelley often doesn't wait to see if the friend wants help before she jumps in to resolve the problem as she sees it.

People respond to being rescued in one of three ways. They may be grateful, they may become resentful because they didn't want help in resolving their problems, or they may become dependent and come to expect the rescuer always to be there to resolve problems. No matter how the friend responds, the rescuer has, in effect, taken on the problems of another, which is not healthy.

3. *You may become a passenger in a relationship.* Rex has become a passenger in any relationship he has had ever since his wife left him. He is not a partner with equal responsibility for making decisions and having input. He simply goes along with whatever the other person wants. He has actually become a burden to his friends because he is so dependent and needs so much approval.

4. *You may become a perfectionist.* In extreme cases, people pleasers don't just want to please others, they want to please them by doing everything perfectly. They spend all of their time not just doing the right things, but doing things just right. They don't make appropriate decisions about relative priorities. *Everything* is a priority. And every detail must be perfect. Consequently, not everything gets done because each thing takes so long. For them, the stress of striving to be perfect will soon become unbearable.

5. *You may become a colluder.* A colluder gives silent permission for someone else to continue

inappropriate behaviors because the colluder won't speak up. Kelley, one of the women who came to one of my seminars, is a colluder. She hates it when her husband jumps in and finishes her jokes, telling the punchline before she can get to it. But she always smiles and laughs along with the others. There are lots of other things Kelley keeps quiet about because she doesn't want to start a fight with her husband, but she is building up resentment inside. Kelley doesn't trust the relationship enough to confront her husband. And in the process, she is teaching him to continue the behaviors which annoy or even hurt her. She thinks she is pleasing him, but she is actually sabotaging the relationship. The resentments will eventually surface.

6. *You may stress out.* People pleasers are so busy working hard at relationships, taking on extra tasks, and being what others want them to be, that they don't always acknowledge the stress they are under. They don't get enough rest. They don't say no to unreasonable demands. They work even when ill. It won't be long before they burn out, stress out, drop out, and give up.

7. *You will never have enough approval.* Though they live a lifestyle based on the exaggerated need for external approval, people pleasers never feel as if they have enough approval. There is always someone else to please. And the approval doesn't last; it can't be banked to use when it's needed next. People pleasers constantly seek to earn more and more approval from others. It is an unending circle of need.

8. *You may sacrifice your standards.* Angela described how she hadn't really wanted to say yes in the back seat of the car that night—she didn't think premarital sex was right. But she was afraid to say no and lose her boyfriend. Later, pregnant and embarrassed, she said "I do" to that same boy because, even

though she didn't want to marry a non-Christian, she didn't want to be an unwed mother. Angela found during her marriage that she said yes to a lot of things she didn't think were right—just to please her husband.

When you are afraid to stand up for what you know is right, you compromise your standards and sacrifice your self-esteem because you know that you really need to make different choices.

9. *You become a liar.* You live a lie when you misrepresent who you are, what you think, what you want, and what is important to you. So if you pretend to love, present yourself to be less than you are, act with a deference you don't feel, affect a blindness to your own needs, or laugh when you really feel like crying, you are lying. And you are lying if you fake beliefs to win approval, go along with others to gain acceptance, assume values you don't agree with to conform, and allow your silence to imply agreement you don't mean.

A healthy self-esteem demands a congruence, an agreement between the self within and the self displayed to others. But if you choose to mislead others as to who you really are, it is because you don't believe that you would be accepted if they knew the real you. This implies that you are not honest and are always worried about being found out.

10. *You are looking to please people rather than God.* A people pleaser spends more time looking around at other people for direction than searching the Word of God for guidelines. It is more important to a people pleaser to be accepted as part of the group than be "accepted in the beloved" (Eph. 1:6). In the eternal scheme of life, the approval of people is of little value.

Unfortunately, becoming a people pleaser does not guarantee that you will get what you want. As you can see from the above dangers, people pleasers usually end up *not* getting the one thing they want most—approval. And in the process, they hurt their own development.

> *What about you? Have you been a victim or a rescuer? Do you always feel you need more approval? Have you repeatedly sacrificed your standards to please someone else?*

THE PSYCHOLOGY OF PEOPLE-PLEASING BEHAVIORS

The theme of people pleasing weaves its way through all forms of human psychology. In *transactional analysis* it is called "the adaptive child." The natural child has urges to explore, to know, to crush, to bang, to express feelings, and to experience all of the pleasant sensations associated with movement and discovery. On the other hand, the child also feels demands from the environment, usually the parents, to curb these basic urges for the perceived reward of parental approval. If Mommy says not to play with the vase in the living room, the child who plays with it anyway and ends up breaking it is punished for being rebellious. The punishment and obvious disapproval in Mommy's voice are enough to make the child think twice about disobeying again. After all, what he or she really wants is Mommy's approval.

This approval, which in many dysfunctional families can disappear as fast as it appears, is an unfathomable mystery to the child who has not yet made any certain connection between cause and effect. All he knows is that he did something Mommy said not to do, and that made Mommy angry. Naturally, the predominant by-product of this process is negative feelings. On the basis of these feelings, a little person raised in a nonnurturing environment concludes, "I'm not okay."

In order to feel okay again, the natural child can be suppressed and the child adapts to the environment— trying to be "good," obeying all of the rules, doing all of the perceived right things, going out of his way to please those in authority, anything to gain approval and feel okay. Children who are good at judging which behaviors will be approved can get the strokes they desire. They also learn that in order to feel okay or to gain approval, they must not do or say what they think or want, but what others think or want. Some children never grow out of this and are still "adaptive children" even as adults.

Ghestalt psychology says that the people pleaser has an ego without a mind, without intentionality of purpose, and without acceptance of his or her own opinions, thoughts, or rationality. The people pleaser seeks to complete the *ghestalt* (the picture) by using the minds (intentionality, purpose, standards) of others. People pleasers feel their personal ideas, opinions, purposes, or goals must be validated by the approval of others. If they are not, they are often discarded as being of no value.

Albert Ellis would say that the people pleaser is clinging to several basic irrational fears, such as:

1. I must be loved and approved of by everyone in my community, especially by those who are most important to me.

2. I must be perfectly competent, adequate, and successful in achieving before I can think of myself as worthwhile.

3. I have no control over my happiness. My happiness is completely in the control of external circumstances.

4. There is one right and perfect solution to each of

my problems. If this is not found, it will be devastating for me.

5. I should be dependent on others and must have someone stronger than myself on whom I can rely.

Behavioral psychologists talk in terms of learned behaviors—actions or words which are immediately followed by reinforcing responses from others or by punishing responses from others. Positively reinforced behaviors are more likely to be repeated. Behaviors which are ignored or punished are usually not repeated frequently in the future. In this sense, the people pleaser's sense of satisfaction and reward is stronger when it comes from outside of the self than from within.

The people pleaser is weak in the area of assertiveness and responsibility, continually letting others make necessary decisions. The passive or nonassertive person is self-denying, inhibited, hurt, and anxious. He or she allows others to choose for him or her, and seldom achieves desired goals. If pushed too far or taken advantage of too often, the nonassertive person attempts to push back—not with assertive skills, for these are nonexistent, but by being aggressive. Hence the term *passive-aggressive.*

The people pleaser's family often did not outwardly express love and acceptance. Risk-taking was not encouraged, and failure was a catastrophe rather than a stepping stone to success. To the child it seemed that love was conditional upon good behavior, and through the dysfunction of a lack of acceptance and self-esteem, the child grew up with a dysfunctional self-concept and manner of relating to others.

People pleasers are basically codependents. They are concerned with being good spouses, parents, friends, or even Christians. They may spend most of their time taking care of others, trying to make them happy. They may put up with abuse, allowing themselves to be taken advantage of. And they usually feel angry and unappreciated for their efforts. They acquiesce to the desires of their spouse, regardless of their own desires. They spend too much of the family budget on toys, clothing, and indulgences for the children. They chauffeur, read to, cook for, clean, cuddle, and coddle those around them, but nobody does for them in return. Most of the time people don't even say thank you. These people feel guilty when they don't live up to the standards and expectations of others. They schedule their priorities around guilt.

Why do they do this? For the fickle approval of others, which is casually given and even more casually taken away. I used to work with a lady named Patti who was a people pleaser. She was well thought of, and people often said that Patti was the best friend anyone could have. No matter what was asked of her, she would take the time to do it, regardless of what else she had going on in her own life. She watched other people's children, although she hated the noise and demands that often accompanied the job. She sewed, cooked, baked, cleaned, and ran errands for most of her friends. Her own chores often did not get completed—or if they did, it was in the middle of the night while the rest of her family slept. One day she realized that if she didn't learn to say no she might lose her family, which she was neglecting, or she might lose her mind trying to juggle all of the commitments she made. The first time she actually said no to a request, the response was predictable, but devastating nonetheless. Some of her "friends" suddenly found new "friends" to take advantage of. They weren't comfortable with this new assertive Patti.

Joyce was another people pleaser, who also was forever ready to do things for other people. Her loyal friends would always berate her for letting "all those other people" take advantage of her, yet they felt quite free to take advantage of her for their own benefit. They gave her approval for doing things for them, but disapproval for doing for others, so their approval was a mixed blessing. While they individually urged her to turn "all those other people" down they never considered withdrawing their own demands.

> *What about you? Have you stifled your natural child? Are you an adaptive child even though you are an adult? Do you seek to use the thoughts, intentions, or rationality of others to guide your decisions? Would you agree that you are codependent in some of your relationships?*

BELIEFS OF A PEOPLE PLEASER

Evaluate your lifestyle. If you haven't already done so, take the self-tests at the beginning of this book. They will give you indications of how you have adapted in the work, social, and romantic areas of your life and give an overall assessment of where you fit on the people pleasing continuum.

Most people will score higher in the *We, You First,* or *You Only* categories. Even if you are basically a *We* person according to the quiz, you may have a few areas in which you are still behaving as a people pleaser. This book will help you find those areas. You may choose to change. You may not. But take a look at the beliefs behind your people-pleasing behaviors.

If you scored high in the *You First* or *You Only* columns on the self-tests, you probably have some of the following beliefs.

1. *I must do everything perfectly.* Actually, you probably judge yourself more harshly than anyone else ever would. You may procrastinate to avoid making

mistakes. You may be chronically late because you spend so much time fussing about your appearance. And you may be excessively anxious about the opinions of others regarding your performance. You may also find that mistakes or minor flaws are distorted in significance. Any criticism is taken as a total rejection of your character. You are probably never satisfied with your appearance or performance.

2. *I should be able to do more.* You are probably always stretching to increase your to-do list for each day. There are already more items on your list for one day than on most people's for a week. But no matter how many things you get done, you tend to focus on those you did not accomplish, or on things you failed to put on the list.

3. *I have to do what people ask me to do.* You may not even see any alternatives to compliance if you are to feel valued and worthy. You are probably doing things for people you don't even like just because it is impossible for you to say no. You probably feel fragmented and tired, and you find you are unable to please anyone because you can't please everyone.

4. *I have to prove myself to everyone else.* You are probably very insecure and want desperately to feel loved, worthwhile, important, and valued. You have already discovered that the need to prove yourself is never met, and you are constantly having to start from scratch to prove yourself in each new situation.

5. *I can make people value me if they need me to do things for them.* You want people to come to depend on you, but you find you have not necessarily earned their approval. In fact, if you give away your time and energies so easily, other people won't respect the value of what you are giving. You have probably already found out that people can count on you and still discount you as a person.

6. I must be everything to everybody. You have set an impossible goal and have already failed, because you cannot possibly be everything to everybody. You are probably already paying the price of experiencing stress overload symptoms because of trying to meet your unrealistic expectations.

If you have identified any of these erroneous beliefs as some you have held, you have already discovered that you cannot live up to these perceptions. You cannot always please people. It doesn't work, and you end up failing to please yourself as well.

> *What about you? Do you try to do everything perfectly? Can you say no to unreasonable demands? Do you try to be everything to everybody?*

ALTERNATIVES TO PEOPLE PLEASING

The approval of others is so conditional, so fragile, and so undependable that we are foolish to base our self-concepts or our sense of worthiness on this approval.

So, what are the alternatives? There are several options. First, we can decide that we will only listen to that inner voice of our self, and do only what we want and what we think is right. Shall we disregard the standards of others, disobey the rules, become rugged individualists? Shall we become a law unto ourselves? No, we must live within the laws of the land in order to continue to have our freedoms. We must behave in ways which are somewhere within the very broad limits of accepted civilized behaviors or be ostracized totally. We must not become aggressive and violate the rights of others.

Besides, because of our sin nature, if we listen only to ourselves and behave accordingly, we are in danger of being separated from God. Prov. 14:12 says,

"There is a way which seemeth right unto a man, but the end thereof *are* the ways of death." Isa. 64:6 says ". . . all our righteousnesses *are* as filthy rags; . . . and our iniquities, like the wind, have taken us away."

A second alternative to a people-pleasing lifestyle is to decide to seek to please God. If we can't please people, if we shouldn't live to please people, and we can't succeed by just pleasing ourselves, then what do we do? Paul says it best when he writes in Gal. 1:10, "For do I now persuade men, or God? or do I seek to please men? for if I yet pleased men, I should not be the servant of Christ" (see also 1 Thess. 2:4). Peter and the apostles refused to follow the high priest and the Sadducees, stating that "We ought to obey God rather than men" (Acts 5:29).

To live in a way that is pleasing to God and fair to ourselves, we must:

- Choose to live by God's standards (John 15:10–11).

- Recognize that we won't be approved of by others all of the time, even if we are approved of by God. The world doesn't really want us to live just for the approval of God. There are plenty of people— even some friends, even some Christians—who want us to break God's laws (John 17:14–17).

- Live intentionally, consciously, and deliberately in accordance with those standards and goals, and experience the abundant life Jesus came to give us (John 10:10).

- Live peaceably with all men, as much as lieth within us (Rom. 12:18).

To accomplish this, we have to rethink our choices. We have to redefine satisfaction, rebuild our self-concepts, deepen our awareness of and relationship to God, and set goals. We must also develop inner strength, abandon our neediness, develop balance in our lives, and regain our personal power. We do this all so we can learn to do for others out of love rather than out of a desperate need for approval.

In the process, we will learn to abandon the bondage we have chosen. In Galatians, Paul tells us to stand fast in the freedom Christ has given us. When we live as people pleasers, we choose to put ourselves in bondage to others. We are trying to serve the wrong masters. Other people aren't to set the standards for us, but God and His Word. We are like Peter, who took his eyes off of the Lord and started to sink in the sea. When we look away from Him for our direction, we can only sink.

It is a tall order. The process will not always be easy or satisfying. But in the long haul, it will be worth it. Life will become exciting, abundant, and free.

2

Review
Your
Relationships

Jeremy was a nice guy. He really was. At work he was bright, innovative, practical, and solution-oriented. He was helpful and supportive, but unafraid to voice a new idea or suggestion. At church Jeremy served in several capacities. He could be counted on to help on work days, fill in as an usher, and sing in the choir. Frequently, he was also the voice of reason at church business meetings when he would stop a rubber stamp vote with a call to consider the question more carefully. He presented well-thought-out facts, reasons, and suggestions. With friends, Jeremy was fun, supportive, and affirming. He also invested in friends by giving of his own ideas and suggestions when appropriate. He was a nice guy.

In marriage, Jeremy was a "super-nice guy." Because his wife was demanding, critical, easily angered, and unconcerned about making public displays which embarrassed Jeremy, he learned, or chose, to become a wife pleaser. He always let his wife choose where to go on vacation, what to do together, and how to spend their money. He let her raise the children her way. He ate whatever she prepared for meals, no matter how she cooked the food. When she would bring up something which might lead to an argument, Jeremy would immediately apologize and agree that she was right. Conflict was avoided at all costs.

"Honey," Jeremy said to his wife one evening, "I've been thinking that I'd like to take an extension course at the university next semester. I'd like to brush up on my writing skills for my job."

"More time away from home? And do you know how much that will cost? Tuition, books, gas, and who knows what else! That's just like you. Plenty of money for a job where they don't appreciate you anyway. If you have all that money, how come you haven't bought me that rocker I've had my eye on for the front room?" his wife retorted angrily.

"Well, gee, Honey! It was just a thought," Jeremy said, giving up one more dream.

Jeremy's wife secretly thought he was a wimp, despising him even while enjoying getting her own way all of the time. Jeremy could tell that in spite of all of his "pleasing" behaviors he was not getting her approval. He consoled himself by telling himself that he was a nice guy.

Sometimes close friends would compliment him on how incredibly nice he was to put up with all of his wife's demanding ways. Even when one friend suggested that Jeremy leave his wife because she was such a shrew, Jeremy merely smiled and shook his head, assuming that his friend was admiring him for his perseverance.

WHO ARE THE PEOPLE PLEASERS?

There seem to be four types of people pleasers: those who seek to please everybody, those who primarily seek to please at work, those who primarily seek to please friends, and those who primarily seek to please a significant other.

Of course, there are combinations of the last three in which people are pleasers in two areas of relationships but not necessarily the third. Let's look more closely at the four primary types.

Those who seek to please everybody

Jane was asked to give a speech at her professional association. It was an honor to have been asked to speak. She prepared well and delivered an informative, interesting, and even humorous speech. She received rave reviews and dozens of sincere compliments. But one person who came up to Jane after the session told her he didn't think that the committee ought to have selected her as the speaker because she didn't have enough experience in the field. Jane was devastated. Even weighted against all the compliments, the criticism still won out.

People in this category are not discriminating about whom they seek to please. They are as concerned about gaining approval from a stranger as they are from a friend or authority figure. They don't want to offend strangers. They don't want to do something wrong in front of a bus boy in a restaurant. They don't want to appear stupid in the cashier's line.

They can't say no to door-to-door salespersons. They smile a lot, not always sincerely. They are eager to serve, but feel pressured by all of the demands upon their time and energies. They don't require that they be treated with mutual respect.

There are rewards for these behaviors. People in this group do get approval at times. And they don't get much criticism, except for when they are doing too much or being too helpful.

There are problems with this approach to life, though, including feelings of being cheated, abused, controlled, bullied, and manipulated. They wonder why people don't like them as much as others who aren't as nice as they are.

> *Are you a people pleaser in all of your relationships? Is it easy for you to say no to people's requests? Do you find yourself striving to please everybody?*

Those who primarily seek to please at work

Some people have developed enough personal security to be *We* people in friendships and at home with family members, but they have not yet overcome their fears of being rejected by authority figures. So they are people pleasers at work.

There are rewards for this pattern. There is a great deal of internal satisfaction gained from accomplishing many tasks, completing a "to-do" list, being able to do more than others, and being self-sacrificing. There can be admiration from peers who tell us they couldn't do as much as we do, or appreciation because we will do the jobs they don't like to do. There can be financial rewards, as well: earned raises, overtime money, and promotions. There can be approval from bosses for jobs well done and for being reliable.

There can also be surprising consequences. We can experience disapproval from peers who feel that we are trying to "butter up" the boss, or that we are trying to steal the glory or show up other workers. There can be a lack of financial rewards as we make ourselves so indispensable that we won't get promoted to a better job. In addition, our personal lives may suffer if we become workaholics and spend too much time at work. Our health may be in jeopardy if the stress continues too long and there isn't sufficient relaxation time allowed.

Do you always do the serving tasks such as setting up rooms for meetings, making the coffee, picking up the doughnuts, performing tasks that are not part of your job? Do you hesitate to make suggestions? Do fellow workers seem to leave some of their tasks for you to do?

Those who primarily seek to please friends

Other people are confident in their abilities to perform on the job and are assertively confrontive when necessary in work situations. They also are secure in one-to-one relationships with significant others because they have learned to trust the relationships and know that their partners will stick by them even through difficulties. But they are not ready to risk rejection by friends. So, in groups or with casual friends, they become people pleasers.

This group of people would identify with Martha, who was busy doing all of the necessary household chores while Mary sat at the feet of Jesus (Luke 10:38–42). Understandably, while glad to be helpful, Martha felt that Mary ought to help as well. The "Marthas" in friendships are the ones who get the meals, do the laundry, run the errands, help with setting up the classrooms, make the coffee, sew the costumes, and perform a thousand other little helpful chores.

Of course, there are rewards for people pleasers who work hard to please friends. Wouldn't *you* like to have a Martha, a helper to free you up to rest, relax, sit at the feet of Jesus, listen to music, or do any number of fun things? We all would. And pleasers are rewarded by being told how wonderful they are and how much we depend upon them. They get the desired approval.

There are also problems. These people pleasers are not appreciated because of *who they are*, but because of *what they do*. Therefore, the approval they get is contingent upon continued pleasing behaviors.

> *Do you ever give negative feedback to a friend? Do you usually go along with whatever others want to do during leisure time? Do you honestly feel as if some of your friends take advantage of you and your good nature?*

Those who primarily seek to please a significant other

I used to work for Helen. Helen was a confident manager at work and a secure friend. She was a *We* person in those roles. However, deep inside she had a pocket of insecurity about being able to keep a man happy. So she had always been very passive in her male-female relationships, becoming more and more of a pleaser as the intimacy of the relationship increased. The more romantically involved she became, the more afraid she was that he would walk away. And the more afraid she was, the more pleasing she became.

One day her fiancé, Russ, had a serious talk with her. "Helen," he said, "I want you to take a good look at yourself. In all other aspects of your life you are self-confident, independent, and assertive. That was one of the reasons I was attracted to you in the first place. But in our relationship that part of you has changed. You are not a partner. You are not the girl I fell in love with. Why not? What happened?"

"I guess I'm afraid if I assert myself with you, you'll leave me," Helen admitted.

Russ reassured her. "I'm not like that. I respect your ideas and opinions. I want to know what you think, feel, and want. Tell me! Okay?"

"I'll try," Helen said.

Helen was able to share with Russ her secret fears of losing him if she did anything wrong or made him angry. Part of that fear stemmed from the fact that her father had left her mother when Helen was only seven. Helen had never seen a man-woman relationship in which there could be constructive disagreement and problems solved together. As a little girl Helen hurt when her father left, and she missed him terribly. She developed a secret belief that all men were like her father—if they didn't get their way, they would leave. As Helen and her fiancé talked, she began to conceive a different set of beliefs about intimate relationships between men and women.

After that, step by tentative step, Helen became more of a *We* person in her relationship with Russ. She became, once again, the person Russ had fallen in love with, and they soon married.

There are rewards in being a pleaser in a romantic relationship. We sometimes get the approval we wish for. But the price we pay for that approval may be complete self-betrayal as we sacrifice who we are in order to become what we think someone else wants us to be. In Helen's case, Russ was insightful and mature enough to share that he wanted a *We* relationship. Unfortunately, many partners aren't knowledgeable enough or courageous enough to verbalize similar requests.

> *Are you assertive with your significant other? Are you free to speak up for yourself in your relationship with your partner? Do you share your ideas, dreams, fears, goals, opinions, and private thoughts with your partner?*

The self-tests at the beginning of the book, when completed and scored, should give you an indication of your people-pleasing tendencies in the different areas of your life. If you have not yet completed them, please take the time to do so now. They should provide helpful, personal insights as you work your way through the rest of this book.

THE ROLE OF GUILT

Inside each of us lives the child we used to be, complete with beliefs, fears, and needs. If that child were deprived of affection and approval, or never felt or accepted parental approval, then he or she may continue to feel guilty for a perceived failure to measure up. The child tries to make up for that failure by becoming a caregiver, a nurturer, or a pleaser.

Most people pleasers feel some degree of guilt, but it is a false guilt. False guilt is feeling self-reproach without having done anything wrong. It is aimed at belittling the self.

When there has been actual wrongdoing, one can experience real guilt—shame when caught and remorse or regret at having made a wrong choice—and seek to obtain forgiveness, correct the wrong, and vow not to repeat the error. The focus in this case is the behavior, rather than the person.

In *The Pleasers: Women Who Can't Say No, and the Men Who Control Them* (Revell, 1987), Dr. Kevin Leman gives several reasons why people pleasers gather guilt:

They feel bad about the past. Whether or not there was wrongdoing, people pleasers have a sense of guilt about the past. Since there is a perception that bad things only happen to bad people, there must be a guilty party. The people pleaser assumes the role.

Monica grew up in a dysfunctional home where her emotional needs were not met. She came to me for counseling one day and told me her story. Although her parents did love her, she did not perceive that they did, so Monica believed herself to be unloved. She was terrified of abandonment and would do anything to earn approval. Monica was sure that she was to blame for her parents' not showing her love.

When questioned, she could not give specifics but mentioned that she used to feel guilty when she would go outside to play and her mother stayed indoors alone. She felt guilty when her father had to work so hard to support the family, so she would not ask for new clothes, shoes, or toys. She felt guilty when her younger sister got hurt in the backyard, as if somehow Monica ought to have been able to stop her sister from climbing onto the picnic table. It was as if anything that happened in Monica's growing up years was her responsibility, her fault. Monica cannot ever remember not feeling guilty.

Monica is now twenty-seven, and her relationships are as dysfunctional as ever. Nothing is too much trouble for her to do for a friend. She is willing to wait for love. She dates emotionally unavailable men for as long as they will stay in the relationship. And she always takes more than her share of the blame or guilt

for anything that goes wrong in a friendship or relationship.

Not often, but every once in a while Monica
gets so tired of carrying around the burden of guilt that
she turns the tables and looks for someone else to blame
for her past, for whatever is happening now, or what
isn't happening that should be. But then Monica slips
quickly back under the burden and reassumes the guilt.

*People pleasers try to live up to the expecta-
tions of others.* Since no one can always meet the
expectations of others, there are plenty of opportunities for people pleasers to feel guilty about not
measuring up—not only in the past, but also in the
present.

Oscar feels guilty any time his boss asks him
a question he can't answer. He works very hard to keep
every possible fact and figure in his head, but as the
business manager of a large company, he can't possibly succeed. The other day Oscar experienced guilt. In
a meeting his boss said, "Oscar, I need detailed information on the water bill to help me make an important
decision on this water conservation plan. What penal-
ties are we being assessed for not meeting our water
conservation goals?"

"About $3,000 a month," Oscar responded.

"What period does the water bill cover?" the
boss asked.

Having just checked the water bill for another
project, Oscar knew the answer. "From the 18th of one
month to the 17th of the next."

"When does the water bill come in? What day
of the month?" the boss asked.

"I don't know," Oscar said.

"But I need to know now," the boss said with
a frown.

Suddenly Oscar felt as if his boss had said
aloud, "Bad boy! Bad boy!" He felt ashamed.

Oscar promised to check out the information and get back to the boss, but he spent the next week hating himself for once again letting his boss down!

People pleasers often feel guilty because they try to live by the standards set by other people. Because the people pleaser automatically gives more credence to the opinions and choices of others than to his own, whenever there is a conflict, the people pleaser automatically assumes he is in the wrong, all of the time.

Rachel has a habit of starting almost every sentence with, "I'm sorry." She assumes that she is interrupting if she has to say something. Since her job is being a secretary to a public utilities board, she is always "interrupting" to deliver a message, to give copies she has been asked to make, to introduce a walk-in visitor, and so on. The board members are tired of hearing Rachel say she's sorry. It is annoying. Rachel feels bad and somehow guilty because she irritates them. It is a vicious cycle for her.

People pleasers would rather suffer than change. They often prefer to go through life feeling guilty than initiate changes in their beliefs, behaviors, and patterns. Feeling guilty may not be pleasant, but it is a familiar bad feeling and one that they have learned to cope with. Change is too scary to consider.

Monica, Oscar, and Rachel all feel false guilt. They feel guilty when they haven't done anything wrong, and they feel guilty about things that are beyond their control. False guilt is a difficult problem to resolve. There is nothing for which to obtain forgiveness. There is no specific person to ask for forgiveness. There is no way to vow to always measure up in the future. Therefore, choosing to live with a sense of false guilt sentences them to a lifelong burden. Their alternative is to choose to develop healthy *We* relationships and to resolve the underlying issues behind people-pleasing behaviors.

> *Do you feel a sense of guilt about your past? Is there some specific act for which you need to seek forgiveness, or do you feel guilty all the time for things beyond your control? Do you feel guilty when you fail to meet the expectations of others?*

LET GO OF FEAR AND GUILT

The next step to overcoming people-pleasing tendencies is to let go of fear and guilt. Sometimes guilt is a way for people pleasers to refuse to admit that they are intimidated by the expectations of others. They may feel angry about what is expected of them, yet they respond by feeling guilty for not meeting those expectations. And since they aren't openly disagreeing with the expectations, their actions appear to acknowledge that others are right. This means that people pleasers choose to pay the price of guilt rather than risk the disapproval of others. Often the child within brings to the adult a sense of guilt for not having measured up, for having been less than perfect, and for not daring to be more or risk more.

To let go of guilt, you must first recognize the feeling of real, honest-to-goodness guilt, not the false guilt you're used to. Then you need to go back to the experience you are reproaching yourself for, and understand that you were doing the best you knew how to survive. Feel compassion for yourself. If you are still living out the choice you made back then, and if that choice is no longer appropriate for your life, then make a different choice for today and the future. Become responsible for your choices, your actions, your priorities, and don't allow people to take that responsibility away from you.

Fear is often a part of a people-pleasing lifestyle. But in order to get on with living as an adult, people pleasers must identify their fears, including the fear of seeming silly, of being rejected, of not being capable, of not being accepted, of failing, or even of succeeding. They must also mentally play out these fears to their extremes and decide if the fears are realistic. Usually, they are not. Unrealistic fears must be discarded. The third step is to learn to "feel" the remaining fears and do what needs to be done. It is fear that keeps all of us from living free.

As one old man said at the end of his life, "My life has been full of trouble, much of which never happened." Don't spend your life worrying about things which may never happen. Learn to let go of those unrealistic fears.

Paul says it well in Phil. 3:13–14. He says that he has not achieved it all yet, but that one thing he has learned is to forget that which was past, to let it go, to look ahead, and to stretch forward toward what is in front. We would all be well-advised to do the same.

PRINCIPLES FOR HEALTHY *WE* RELATIONSHIPS

When taking a look at your relationships to discover possible people-pleasing patterns, you may want to keep the following principles in mind.

The past can be resolved. The past has an undeniable influence on your present and even your future. However, that influence need not be negative. To keep the influence positive, look at a current problem, decide if it has its roots in past experiences or decisions, and then make a new choice about how to behave or think. Understanding the past can help you make a proper decision.

Remember Monica, who always felt guilty? When she came to the point of wanting to change her lifestyle, she talked openly about her past. Encouraged to think through past experiences, she was surprised to discover that her guilt feelings had no real basis in fact. She was not a bad little girl for going outside to play and leaving her mother alone inside the house. It was not her fault that her dad had to work so hard; in fact, she realized that her father had a problem with handling money. If he wanted something, he went out and bought it, so they were always in debt and always behind in their payments. She saw, for the first time, that most of the guilt she experienced and carried around with her was false guilt. She learned to ask herself three questions each time she started to feel guilty.

- Am I doing something specific which is wrong?
- Who says it is wrong?
- Why is what I am doing wrong?

Monica laughs when she tells about this process. "Usually the answer I get to the first question is that I am not *pleasing* someone, anyone. And the person who says I am wrong is usually just myself. The reason I think I am wrong is that I am differing from someone else, or my needs are in conflict with the desires of someone else's. Since I am not a bad person, I am not usually doing something which is morally wrong or hurtful to someone else."

It is a slow process for Monica to change a lifetime habit of automatically assuming feelings of guilt for everything uncomfortable in her life, but she is working on it—and is having success.

Remember Zacchaeus, from Luke 19:1–10? He had been a tax collector for the Romans and had become rich. When he met Jesus, Zacchaeus took a look at who he had been in the past, and made some new decisions. He decided to give away half of his fortune to the poor and to restore fourfold to anyone he may have cheated. Jesus affirmed his decision, and not only his right to change, but also his ability to change. As Zacchaeus found out, it is never too late to change.

We train people how to treat us. The way people treat us is largely based on how we have taught them to relate to us. For example, if people continue to take advantage of us, we usually have let them, and probably have encouraged this behavior. If they continue to abuse us, it is because we have trained them to believe it is okay to do so. If a coworker frequently leaves her work for you to do, it's probably because you have repeatedly done her work for her when she "didn't have time" or "didn't get around to doing it," so she knows you will do it again.

On the other hand, if people seem to respect us, it is because in one way or another we have required mutual respect in the relationship. If people are friendly and kind to us, it usually means that we have also set that tone in our relationships (see Prov. 27:19).

We relationships are open, honest, and caring. Therefore, when building *We* relationships, you need to be prepared to be open, honest, and caring. Being open means being willing to share your ideas, opinions, and preferences. You need to speak out on issues and yet be vulnerable to the honest feedback from others. Being honest means being willing to let people see who you really are and not withholding negative responses, even if they conflict with what someone expects of you. It also means being willing to confront if necessary, trusting the relationship to survive difficult times. Being caring includes being willing to risk being the first to express love, affection, and approval.

Whenever I think of confronting, I think of the story of King David and the prophet Nathan. What a situation to be in! God sent Nathan to tell King David that he, the king, had sinned. David could have had Nathan killed for daring to criticize him. Yet Nathan, choosing to please God rather than a man, boldly confronted David saying, unforgettably, "Thou art the man!" (2 Samuel 12:7). What courage!

Pleasing others should be a matter of choice, not habit. There is an element of pleasing others in all *We* relationships, but it is not at the expense of self, values, or ethics. Instead, it is a matter of mutual caring and respect. It is a matter of making a specific choice to do for or give to another person *because we want to* at that moment. Giving joy or pleasure is the goal rather than earning approval. Giving becomes an expression of caring and love.

In Gal. 6:2–5, Paul encourages us to do two things. He encourages each of us to carry our own burden, and he encourages us to bear the burdens of one another. This implies that there ought to be a mutual respect between parties in a relationship, and that good relationships are not one-sided—they are based on sharing.

When you are considering whether or not to please others, take these steps:

- Ask yourself who it is you are trying to please. Be sure you know if you are trying to please a specific person, or just being pleasing in general.

- Ask yourself if the behavior you are contemplating will actually please that person or if you are just assuming that it will please him or her. Then verify your assumptions to see if they are valid.

- Ask yourself why you want to please this person. Maybe you are feeling kind and want to go out of

your way today to be extra nice. Or are you trying
to earn reciprocal approval?

- Ask yourself if you really want to do this thing you
are contemplating. If you don't, then carefully consider the probable consequences of not doing
whatever it is, and make a choice to either do it or
not.

If you want to do something to please someone, then acknowledge to yourself that you are choosing
to do it for yourself and not because you are trying to
win approval.

*Pattern the relationship after that of Christ and
the church.* Paul gives us a beautiful model to follow when
building relationships (Eph. 5:21–32). He says we ought
to consider Christ's example. Christ gave up His status
in heaven to walk an earthly journey with us. He gave up
His life to pay for our salvation. He currently spends His
time making daily intercession for us with the Father, as
a High Priest who understands the temptations we face
and sometimes give in to, and as an attorney who argues
for mercy for us (see Heb. 4:14–16; I John 2:1). Christ did
not *have* to give us anything. He chose to. He did it so
that our joy would be full (John 10:10, 15:11).

Expect the change to be uncomfortable at first.
Making any change is uncomfortable, even a good
change. Taking on a long-awaited and desired promotion at work involves learning new behaviors, new
information, and new routines. Starting an exercise program is uncomfortable at first as unfamiliar muscles
are stretched and toned. Just so, making a lifestyle
change will be uncomfortable.

People have been used to your behaving a certain way. When you start changing, there will be some
who will not reinforce the change. They want the
familiar you back. They want to continue taking

advantage of you. It's easier for them if you do not speak up. You will be tempted to slip back into people-pleasing behaviors to regain their approval. *Anticipate the temptation, and do not give in to it.* We are promised that for whatever temptation we experience, there will be a way of escape provided by God (1 Cor. 10:13).

There will be people in your life who will not believe that you are sincere when you begin to make changes. They will be skeptical, much as the Jewish Christians were unwilling to believe that Saul the persecutor had become Paul the evangelist (Acts 8:1–3; 9:1–29).

If you have been a people pleaser for a long time, you are familiar with the patterns you have followed. The new routines will be different and difficult to remember at times. You will not be comfortable with conflict, confrontation, standing up for yourself, going against the crowd, or saying no. Understand that you will be uncomfortable. Be prepared for it, and determine to live through it. Develop a "comfort zone" with the new habits by practicing them over and over. The more you practice, the easier they will become.

Seek to gain God's approval. The most important relationship in your life is your relationship with God. His is the approval you will want to seek with all of your heart, soul, and mind (Matt. 22:37).

Other people are not the proper primary source of love, approval, acceptance, and validation in our lives. These things should come first from God, and then from ourselves. What we get from others is a bonus, not something we should strive to build our lives around.

When we look to others for love, applause, or approval, we give those others power over us. We think they can withhold their approval from us if we do not act in the ways they want us to. We feel that they love us conditionally, based on whether or not they are pleased with our behavior. In response to these feelings we either become dependent, or we go to the other extreme and become too independent, saying, "I don't have to please anyone—that way they can't control me." Neither is a pleasant lifestyle. You either become addicted to people who are nice to you, or you become possessive, jealous, greedy, and irritating.

We often compete for love and approval. Because we think there isn't enough to go around, we want to knock others out of the way to keep them from receiving what we think is our share.

We don't do this when we build our lives around seeking and obtaining approval from God— when we pattern our lives around the principles in God's Word. When we become conformed to the image of Christ Jesus, His Son, we become the people God designed us, individually, to be.

Sheila decided to build her life around seeking God's approval. She took Gal. 5:22–23 as her guide and focused on developing in her life the characteristics of love, joy, peace, patience, meekness, goodness, gentleness, self-control, and faith. Every day for a month Sheila practiced doing loving things. She recorded what she did each day in a journal. She did a Scripture word study on love. She read a couple of books on Christian *agape* love.

The second month she added joyful behaviors and attitudes. Each day she affirmed the joy in her life. She discovered many sources of joy she had taken for granted before. Her Scripture study and outside reading that month focused on joy. The third month she worked on becoming peaceful in her heart.

By the end of the ninth month, Sheila had completed intensive Scripture studies on each of the characteristics in those verses, had practiced the behaviors on a daily basis, and had become more mature in her spiritual walk with Christ.

You could use any number of Scriptures for your guideline to a lifestyle that is pleasing to God. Some places to start include 2 Pet. 1:5–8; John 15:1–15; and Eph. 4:29–32.

Rom. 8:29 says that before the foundations of the world, God preordained that we should become "conformed to the image of his Son." Studying the life and characteristics of our Lord Jesus Christ and working at becoming more like Him will give you a wonderful foundation for the lifestyle changes you want to make.

3

Identify
Your
Challenges

Harley told me that he remembers very clearly being eight years old. That was the year he got his first bicycle, met George Powell (who became his best friend for years), lost his dog, and vowed never to be lazy.

One evening when Harley was eight, his dad came home angry and spent the next few hours yelling at the family, making everyone feel miserable. It seemed an employee at work had missed a big order and lost a major client for the company because he had been too lazy to take care of business. "I'll kill that lazy bum!" Harley's dad raved. The impact on the company was significant, and in the next few months the family experienced a need to tighten the financial belt in order to make ends meet. Harley remembers deciding that he would never be lazy. He didn't ever want to be on the receiving end of his father's anger. He didn't want to be killed. He didn't want to be broke. And he didn't want his family to suffer financially.

So Harley grew up to be an industrious, hard-working adult. He was always considered the best employee one could find because Harley always took care of business. Harley was great.

The only problem was that Harley did all of this based on an eight-year-old's decision. Therefore, his perspective on life was that of a child rather than an adult. The result was that Harley could never decide to just relax. He could never put off anything until the next day—even if it wasn't a top priority. Instead, Harley worked every day to the absolute fullest. "Everything must be done today" was his motto. If anything ever was left for the next day, it was because Harley was either sick or he simply ran out of time, even though he often didn't leave work until ten at night. Otherwise, he did it all.

Other people might admire him, but many of his friends just shake their heads and say, "That's Harley!" They leave him alone to do his work. No one will ever say Harley is lazy. They do say that Harley is driven, likely to have a heart attack, and needs to relax and take life less seriously.

One day Harley may look at the way he is living out his decision to not be lazy. If he were to examine his lifestyle, he would acknowledge that he is not lazy. Quite the opposite, he usually does too much. Somewhere between the extremes lies a whole world of choices Harley could make. But those choices are only available to him as a rational adult. As long as he is letting the child within make his decision, he will continue to work himself to death.

THE CHILD WITHIN

Many people-pleasing behaviors come from the child who still lives within us—the child we once were. For many of us, the experiences, decisions, and hurts which shaped the child continue to govern our adult lives today. That child is a part of us and will always be there. That child was a courageous person, doing whatever he or she thought was needed to survive.

It is important to recognize and not to disown that child within. We should not be like Harley, who has not let the child within mature. Harley has become a people pleaser because of an inadequate child within— a child who was reacting to his world, believing that others would not accept him if they knew him as he really was. Harley's self-concept is low. He does not live consciously or make choices for himself. He instinctively responds to the expectations of others.

With every daily decision there is a conflict between the child within and the adult. As we consider the children we once were, we may remember pain, rage, fear, embarrassment, or humiliation. We may respond by repressing, disowning, repudiating, or forgetting who we were and why we made the decisions we did. We actually reject that child within, just as others rejected us. Thus, we never allow the child to mature. But by nurturing the child within, by being understanding and caring toward ourselves, we allow for growth to occur, growth which may have been stunted for years.

An adult who mindlessly lives out the decisions made by the child within is actually unable to grow toward maturity in those areas of life. Left rejected, abandoned, misunderstood, and unrecognized, the child can turn into a troublemaker. Accepted, recognized, and embraced, the child can enhance our lives.

My friend Emily tells about a time she begged for something from her teacher. She pleaded until the irritated teacher finally gave in. But when she got what she had wanted so much, Emily felt terrible because she had made her teacher unhappy. Emily was fearful that her favorite teacher wouldn't like her any more. So Emily decided as a six-year-old never to ask for anything from anyone again.

Emily lived out that promise to herself. She never asked anyone for anything. But this decision became a hindrance to her adult development. She couldn't stop and ask for information when she was lost. She often hurt her back lifting heavy boxes at work because she would not ask for help. She worked late to finish her typing assignments while other secretaries in the office had plenty of free time because she would not ask for assistance. In addition to never asking for things, or maybe because of that, Emily never learned to be a good receiver. She hated for someone to offer assistance. She hated to be given gifts. She did not accept help. "I can do it myself," she always said.

At last, Emily was confronted by a friend about her problem with asking and receiving. She acknowledged that she had a problem that she would like to resolve. She sought counseling and began to sort through the issues. As Emily discovered where the lifestyle originated, she was able to choose to look at each situation and decide if asking for something was the reasonable choice to make. She would not lose respect— or her friends—by asking for assistance, information, and directions.

At the age of twenty-seven, Emily decided to begin risking (and for her it was a risk) by beginning to ask. Whenever she felt the familiar anxiety inside about asking for something, she was gentle with herself and reminded herself that the person being asked would not reject her as a person, even if the request was not granted. With practice, Emily became more comfortable asking for what she truly needed. She did not lose her independence. Emily decided that she did indeed enjoy doing things for herself. She liked working hard. She liked the challenge of trying to race against the clock to complete an assignment. She still made some decisions not to ask for help. That was her choice. But now she was making the decision as an adult, not as a child.

Often the child within is afraid to speak out for fear of being rejected or punished. So, even as adults, we may be afraid to speak up, to be honest, to express opinions, to confront, or to refuse even unreasonable requests. The adults we are today, bound by the child within, may be afraid to risk reaching out or initiating contact, afraid to give and receive compliments or to show love and affection. The challenge is to take back control of our lives. To do this, we must recognize and nurture the child within, begin to make adult choices, and set and achieve goals.

To recognize and acknowledge your child within, take a few minutes to complete these sentences.

- When I was a child I tried to please . . .

- The person I most wanted to please was . . .

- The ways I pleased that person was to . . .

- When I pleased that person I felt . . .

- The ways I continue to try to please that person (or others like him or her) are . . .

- The person I could never please was . . .

- The ways I tried to please that person were . . .

- When I couldn't please that person, I . . .

- The ways I am still trying to please that person (or others like him or her) are . . .

- I remember making decisions as a child to . . .

All of us have unresolved issues from childhood which color our lives as adults. One of the first
steps to overcoming a tendency to be a people pleaser
is to try and resolve some of those issues.

As I look back over my growing up years, it's
easy for me to see how much of a textbook case I was
as a people pleaser. But at the time, all I was concerned
about was getting people to like me and approve of me
at any cost.

As a little girl I was always trying to please
my dad. I never felt as if I succeeded. I can't remember
ever receiving a direct compliment from him. Actually,
I do remember him saying once, "Why can't you always
behave like you did tonight?" This meant, I assumed,
that I had done well that night. However, the good feeling I had from the "compliment" was overshadowed by
the message that I didn't always measure up.

Being sent to my room or spanked was nothing compared with the worst punishment Daddy could
administer, a sad shake of his head and the words, "I'm
very disappointed in you." Devastated, I would vow
never to let him down again. I was constantly developing a new set of impossible standards for myself. I had
to be perfect. I had to please. No matter what it cost
me in time, energy, effort, or even a sacrifice of myself,
I had to try harder for approval.

I wanted so desperately to belong. As a small
child I took it upon myself to *make* people like me. Unfortunately, I never felt I received enough approval from
my peers or from adults in my young life. I remember
giving my friends my favorite toys. I was trying to buy
their friendship. But the next day they would be playing with someone else—*with my toys!*

I behaved at school. I studied hard. I practiced
my handwriting. I made good grades. I tried to be the

ideal student. Instead of going out at recess, I stayed inside to help the teacher, desperately waiting for approval. All I remember was being shooed out to the playground.

As I grew up I became even more of a people pleaser. I was more concerned about doing what other people thought I should do than what I thought I should do. My own assessment didn't hold the same value as the evaluation of others. I was terrified of disapproval and criticism. In particular, I tried to seek approval from the male authority figures in my life as a replacement for the acceptance I didn't feel from my father.

In graduate school I tried to "read" the instructors and see how to best get an A. And I always got A's, except in one class where I misjudged the instructor's expectations. I noticed that he would argue with any opinion expressed in class. He would seem to ridicule that person publicly. I didn't want to be rejected, so I seldom spoke out in class. I relied on my research papers and my test scores to earn my A. My written work did get A's, so I was shocked when I got a C on my report card. I called the instructor and requested an explanation. "Well," he said, "you didn't participate in class. You could have contributed a lot, but you didn't, so you earned a C." He wouldn't change my grade. Once again, I hadn't measured up to the expectations of a male authority figure. I was crushed.

At work, I became the one who always said yes to any request for help, regardless of the consequences to my own needs, schedule, or energy level. I worked overtime every chance I got, even if I didn't get paid for it. I volunteered to do extra assignments, wanting to be the one people could count on. But one day my boss took me aside and told me that I shouldn't try to hog the overtime hours or look as if I were an "apple polisher." Once again, I had failed to earn the approval I so desperately wanted.

At church, I was the first to arrive and help at a social, and the last person to leave after every dish had been washed and the floor swept clean. No matter how tired I was from working, I could always be counted on to help out. I not only went the second mile, but usually the next five, as well.

I was the submissive partner in relationships, rarely voicing my opinions, always going along with whatever the other person wanted. In my attempts to please the people in my world, I lost touch with myself and my own needs and wants. The only need I was aware of in myself was to belong, to be accepted.

By the time I was twenty-seven, I found myself watching television shows I didn't like, eating food I didn't enjoy, going places I'd rather not, pretending to be someone I wasn't. I was always deferring to other people. I had come to admit secretly—only to myself, of course—that life was basically unfair. I was the one who gave too much, loved too much, and backed down too often. I was the one people took for granted. I felt ripped off, cheated, and used. But I kept my insecurities and exaggerated fears of criticism and rejection well-masked. I hid my hurt, swallowed my pride, and wore a bright smile. But I lived in constant fear of being found out.

And then one day I was. I had just started to work in my first office job. Right away a guy named Steve noticed me and began stopping by my desk occasionally to chat. I enjoyed the attention. One day I was in the cafeteria on my break when he came over to my table and asked if he could sit down. Smiling up at him, I nodded.

"You are really a nice person," he began. Immediately I looked around for something to *do* for him to keep this approval coming my way. I asked if I could get him a cup of coffee or a muffin. "No," he replied. "I don't want you to *do* anything for me. Let's just talk."

That made me nervous. I didn't know how to just *be* with someone. Steve noticed my nervousness and asked what was the matter. I laughed a bit deprecatingly, and confessed that I felt as if I should be doing something for him.

Steve took my comment as an opportunity to give me some feedback. He literally reached inside my mask and touched my inner self. He said he had noticed that I worked very hard to be nice, and began calling into question my people-pleasing behaviors. He said I was a nice person, and didn't have to work so hard at acting nice. He said he thought I was making wrong choices.

His criticism hurt (after all, he was one of the people whose approval I wanted), but I sensed the truth in what he was saying. I asked him to tell me more and I listened carefully, hoping for guidance on how to change. He said that he thought I was so busy trying to please people that it didn't seem as if I had time to become the person God had created me to be. He asked if I had sought God's approval. That was a sobering question! He challenged me to relax and to be a real person, the person I was inside. He said that people could like me for who I was rather than just for what I did for them.

Finally, I saw what I had become—a child within an adult body, going around trying to earn "Daddy's" approval, but never feeling successful. Oh, most of my bosses considered me a super employee. I was promoted quickly to positions of significance in my career. I was rewarded in many ways, but I was never satisfied because what I really wanted (my father's approval) wasn't what I was getting. You see, *you never get enough of what you really don't want!* All of the approval of all of the men in the world would never have satisfied the child within me, because that wasn't what I really wanted.

I was scared, but I was also very tired of working so hard to please others and not ever feeling as if I were succeeding. I was ready to try to escape from my self-made prison. I agreed to try and make changes.

Steve and I talked almost every day after that. I told him about my experiences with trying to stop earning the approval of others. Sometimes I succeeded, sometimes I fell back into the old routines.

The first time I said, "I'm sorry, but no," the response was both predictable and painful.

"What's happened to you? You used to be such a sweet person!"

Yes, I almost caved in at that criticism, and I wanted to retreat into my former behavior to win back that approval. But somewhere within me a voice warned that if I backed down now, I would never escape the lifelong pattern I had established. I found the strength to stand my ground.

I only knew Steve for thirty days before he quit his job to travel through Europe. But he was one of the people God has brought into my life at important times to stand at critical crossroads and point me in the right direction. He helped me choose the right fork in the road, and my journey from pleasing others to learning to please God—and in the process, be true to myself—was begun.

I was still cooperative, still productive, still a hard worker, but more and more I made those choices because that was the kind of person *I wanted me to be* and because that was the kind of person I believed *God wanted me to be*. I no longer acted that way to earn the approval of someone else.

The journey was not completed overnight. Actually, I'm still on the road. It has taken miles of baby steps and years of practice, learning first just who I was and then sharing myself with others. Sometimes I get approval, and that's nice. Sometimes I don't, and that's not fun. But I've learned that it is also not the end of the world. When I get that negative feedback, I can stop and reevaluate. Maybe I do need to rethink a decision, or choose another behavior. But I may also choose not to make a change. The nice thing is that *the choice is mine*, and I must take responsibility for who I am and what I do.

Basically, I have made a lot of progress. But sometimes when I am overworked, when I am sick or exhausted, I still have a tendency to slip back into the familiar pattern of looking outside for the approval rather than within and above.

My story has another chapter. Several years after I had consciously decided to work on no longer seeking my father's approval, my parents came to live with me. At the time I was the administrator of a state hospital where over a thousand developmentally disabled residents lived. The level of responsibility was tremendous and varied. The one-hundred-year-old facility presented major challenges as we tried not only to hold it together, but also to ensure that it met all safety codes. And we tried to make it homelike and attractive.

Dad often said, "I don't see how you do it! I could never do what you do. You are terrific! "

Finally, at age thirty-nine, the child within got what she wanted. Dad was pleased.

It was healing. It was nice. It was good to hear. It was appreciated. But, interestingly enough, I discovered that Dad's approval was no longer the motivating force in my life. It had taken its rightful place. My approval, and God's approval, was actually more important to me. It was a freeing experience.

Are there some decisions you made as a child that you are living out today? What decisions did you make as a child that, as an adult, you would make again? What decisions did you make as a child that, as an adult, you would change?

MAKING ADULT DECISIONS

If you are living out a childhood decision or letting the child within keep you from fully experiencing life, you may want to ask yourself four questions.

1. *Do I respond instinctively to situations, or do I make conscious choices?* Often the instinctive response comes from the child within. Conscious choices are the prerogative of a mature adult.

A couple years ago I went out to the shooting range to qualify on several weapons, a requirement for my job as associate warden in a state prison. I did just fine with the revolver and the rifle. But when they handed me the shotgun, I experienced an instinctive panic inside. I had just attended the class on using the shotgun. I had watched others shoot. I couldn't understand my panic. My breathing became short and labored. My hands became cold and sweaty. I was afraid of the shotgun. The instructor stood by, gently talking me through the steps of firing the shotgun. "Breathe deeply. Relax. Hold the gun tightly against your shoulder. Breathe deeply. Ease the trigger back," he coached.

I fired the gun and gratefully handed it back to the rangemaster. But I was puzzled. Why was I so afraid of the shotgun?

That night I thought back to my childhood and remembered that my father used to go hunting. One year the whole family went with him. As a young child, I had found the sound of the shotgun frightening. I had covered my ears as my dad shot duck after duck. The fear was explained.

The next day I returned to the range. "I won't let this gun frighten me!" I asserted to the rangemaster. "I am an adult. I am not a little girl. There is nothing to fear." Taking the shotgun, I went to the firing line and shot without a problem. It was an example of conscious choice versus instinctive response.

2. Am I clear about my decisions and choices, or do I experience a degree of vagueness? The child within often lacks a clear picture of the facts, choices, consequences, and alternatives involved in life situations. The mature adult can usually sort these out. If you are confused about an issue, even after researching it and considering the alternatives, you may be operating from the child within.

In Coleen's family love was expressed by buying things. When her parents wanted to show affection, they bought gifts. Any good deed was rewarded with money. Coleen grew up thinking that if someone liked her, they would give her something. She has grown into an adult who is always in serious debt because she "treats" herself by buying things, even when she can't afford them. When she is depressed, she buys something. When she is lonely, she goes shopping. When she is trying to make friends, she buys them gifts. But Coleen also expects her friends to spend money on her as a sign that she is worthy and valued, too.

Recently Coleen took a hard look at the way she related to money. She realized that she was living with a childish, distorted perspective about the significance of money in relationships. She has built a financial plan which will have her out of debt within the next two years. She is finding ways of expressing love and affection in relationships other than by giving gifts. She has also quit expecting expressions of affection toward her to be financial in nature.

3. Am I willing to risk or afraid to risk? Frequently, we find that the child within is afraid of risking, afraid of rocking the boat or being rejected. A person may continue a dependent lifestyle and never develop a healthy sense of independence.

The mature adult can evaluate a situation and make a considered decision to risk. As adults we need to be honest with ourselves about who we are and what we have become. Persons unable to do this experience self-denial and refuse to take an honest look at themselves.

When my best friend, Dotti, was a little girl, she was her father's darling. Then her brother was born when she was about eighteen months old. Very quickly she understood that she was no longer the baby, no longer the darling. As the months passed, she felt as if she hated her little brother. She was very angry with him. When she was three, she and her brother both became ill and had to be hospitalized. Her brother died. Dotti was frightened. She imagined that she had somehow killed her little brother because she had been angry with him.

Although she suppressed the reason for her fear, Dotti grew up afraid to express her anger because of the terrible consequences. She was the peacemaker in the family of four feuding siblings. She was the "good child" in school. She grew up with all of the classic behaviors of a people pleaser. She had a lot of anger inside, but wasn't skilled in confronting. She would simply stuff her anger inside until it erupted uncontrollably. She was always afraid to be open, honest, or caring in relationships with men for fear that they would leave her. It wasn't until she was forty-nine years old that she got in touch with the cause of her fear of expressing anger. She realized that all of her life she had been afraid that her anger would "kill" the relationships in her life. At last she was able to begin making changes.

4. Are you able to be honest? The child within may have an idea that something isn't right, but often that child is unable to face the reality of a situation and retreats into a fantasy world, hoping things will turn out all right. The child takes no responsibility for initiating a change. This is a passive orientation toward life.

The mature adult has learned that respect for the truth may involve confrontation. It may require standing up for an unpopular cause, and it may mean dealing with unpleasant reality in lieu of an idyllic fantasy.

A radio show in San Diego often announces birthdays and anniversaries. There is a standing joke that when they announce an anniversary, like "Jane and Joe have been married five years today," they add, ". . . and in all those years they've never had a fight!" There are some marriages where that is true—not because there has never been a disagreement between the parties, but because one or both of the people have failed to speak up, confront, or attempt to resolve the problems. The relationship is being lived as a fantasy rather than a reality.

Once we have looked at our behavior to identify the decisions made as children that we are still living out as adults, we can identify the changes that need to be made. Paul says in 1 Cor. 13:11 that when he was a child he thought as a child, understood as a child, and spoke as a child. However, since becoming a man, he learned to put away childish things.

Who we were and how we behaved as children was fine for then. We made the best choices and decisions we felt we could with the "givens" we faced. However, now that we are adults, it is time to put away childish things. It is time to grow up.

A QUESTION OF SELF-ESTEEM

The overall challenge is for you to raise your self-esteem. But each step along the way is a challenge in itself. First, you must find the beginning. The journey may be a bit painful as you retrace your steps to the child within. Next you must decide to make changes.

Taking a risk, any risk, is a big challenge to a people pleaser. The next challenge is getting out from under guilt and fear and acknowledging who you are and what your needs are. After that, your hurdle is to decide which areas of your life you want to change.

In the process, you begin to rebuild your concept of who you are, and you develop a self-esteem that will let you be the person God designed you to be—with or without the applause of others. Independence is a virtue of self-esteem.

You must acknowledge your own needs and recognize that you are a worthy individual. You must value yourself in order to have self-esteem. This means that you must bring your inner self into line with the outer self you portray. Self-esteem requires congruence. The self within and the self without must be the same. If you are hiding behind a mask, you will not have high self-esteem. Because you are afraid people will not value you, you hide who you think you are. You need to be honest about what you know, how you feel, and what you want, desire, or need. And you need to accept your right to experience those feelings; not doing so is self-denial and repression.

As human beings we tend to base our concepts of self more on input from other people than on how God sees us. In fact, many Christians often give more weight to the input from other people than they do to the spiritual basis for positive self-esteem.

There is a *functional* basis for self-esteem which has three aspects. They are *appearance* (how well we look), *performance* (how well we do), and *status* (how well others think of us). Basing our self-concepts on this functional basis makes us productive; it gives us incentives to achieve, makes us contribute to the world, and makes us doers rather than observers. It makes life exciting. Progress and growth are measurable.

To some degree we all use the functional basis as a foundation for our self-concepts. As a result, we can increase our esteem by

- setting and achieving specific goals
- getting a better job
- learning a new skill or hobby
- perfecting an existing skill or hobby
- getting involved in serving others in ministry or in the community
- doing one kind thing for someone else each day.

However, there are problems with using this criteria as the sole basis for self-esteem. We tend to become competitive, workaholics, or overachievers. We emphasize *doing* over *being*. When even minor setbacks or failures occur there is a loss of self-esteem.

On the other hand, using a *feeling* basis for self-esteem would require us to base our self-esteem on the way we feel about ourselves at a given moment. The feeling basis primarily focuses on the level of belonging, worthiness, and competence we feel. This can be beneficial to some degree. Our feelings are valid indicators of what is going on in our world, and we ought not to ignore them. In fact, depending upon our own feelings for how we view ourselves tends to make us independent and allows us to be "true" to ourselves. If we want to strengthen our self-concepts in the area of feelings, we might

- focus on good feelings
- try to be around people who make us feel good
- choose to be happy
- develop positive self-talk.

But if we have unrealistic expectations, we won't feel very good about ourselves when we don't live up to them. Our feelings may be based on *perceived* input from others rather than on *fact*. For example, we may think that we are being ignored, when in reality someone didn't see us. Basing our self-concepts on feelings has serious drawbacks.

Sometimes we try to base our self-esteem on a "feedback" basis. This means we must depend on what others think and say about us, on their level of acceptance, for our sense of well-being.

The approval of others is important in that it tells us if we are behaving in a socially accepted manner. And in some areas of life it is appropriate to care about how others perceive us. Good friends can give us excellent feedback about how we are doing in our personal and spiritual growth. If we want to increase the esteem we experience based on feedback from others, we might try

- soliciting feedback from good friends
- remembering compliments
- getting "hugs" from people we know like us
- spending time with people who like and respect us.

However, sometimes the feedback from others is biased. It can be tinged with envy, jealousy, or even malice. Someone else's opinion of who you ought to be or what you ought to do may not be the same as God's. So depending on the feedback of others has its drawbacks, too. In addition, the feedback you get from others will differ from person to person, and even the feedback you receive from the same person may vary from day to day. You could go crazy trying to please everyone all of the time.

Remember Noah? It's a good thing he did not base his self-esteem on the feedback of others. He was undoubtedly the laughingstock of the town! No one had ever heard of a flood before. They saw no reason to build a boat unless you were going to sail it on a large body of water.

A better basis for self-esteem would be to consider how God views us and consider His esteem of us. Studying His relationship with us can assist us in valuing ourselves and help us to develop a positive self-esteem. If God accepts us, forgives us, loves us, and fellowships with us, can we possibly consider ourselves unworthy?

Suppose a famous person, an actor or a billionaire or a world-renowned musician, treated you the way God does. How would you feel about yourself? Wouldn't you feel important? If someone you admire and respect were to seek you out, spend his most valuable possession on you, give up his life for you, promise to always be with you, affirm you, defend you, and fellowship with you, wouldn't you feel pretty good about yourself? That's exactly how God shows His love for us. Look at His relationship with us:

- God designed us (Ps. 139:13–16).

- God knows us (Ps. 139:1–12; Heb. 4:12–13).

- Jesus understands us (Heb. 4:14–16).

- God accepts us (Eph. 1:6).

- God loves us (John 3:16; Jer. 31:3; Rom. 8:38–39).

- God values us (1 Pet. 1:16–20).

- Jesus defends us (1 John 2:1–2).

- God forgives us (1 John 1:9–10; Matt. 6:14–15).

- Jesus fellowships with us (1 John 1:3–7).

- God gives to us (James 1:17; Luke 11:10–13).
- God enables us (Eph. 4:8–16; Rom. 12:5–10).
- God comforts us (2 Cor. 1:3–5).
- Jesus stays with us (Matt. 28:20).

If we want to increase our self-concepts based on God's view of us, we will choose to:

- recognize how God sees us
- accept that His perspective is correct
- ask His input on areas in which to grow
- be obedient in our walk
- keep a clear conscience
- treat others as we want to be treated
- keep our relationship with God current and personal.

There is a principle of reciprocal causation which says that behaviors that generate good self-esteem are also expressions of good self-esteem, and expressions of good self-esteem also generate good self-esteem.

Getting Started

You can start any time. Decide if the child within you is crying out to be recognized, nurtured, and freed from making the decisions for the adult you are today. Identify which choices you need to examine more closely and which choices you want to change. Shore up the foundation of your self-esteem. Develop a plan to become all you can be. The remaining chapters in this book are specifically designed to assist you in developing the skills needed to speak up, reach out, and love life. Start with whatever chapter you think might benefit you the most.

Part II

Speak Up—
Become More
Honest

4

Express Your Opinions

Cathryn had a problem. She was the director of a school for the developmentally disabled. At one time the school building had been used as a mental asylum, but that was decades ago. Most people in the community, however, didn't know the difference between mental illness and developmental disability. There was little support for the school except from the parents and relatives of the students.

The school needed community support. It needed funds, favorable legislation, good stories in the press, and positive regard. What could be done to educate the community? Cathryn brought up the question during a staff meeting. The challenge was so big that at first the responses were a bit outlandish.

"We could go door to door and tell people about us," someone suggested.

"Skywriting!"

"Billboards!"

"You could get on one of those local talk shows and tell about the work we do here," a woman ventured.

"We could make everyone in the community spend a day here to see what we are all about!" one staff member offered jokingly.

Cathryn laughed at the image of a local bank president sitting in a classroom with the developmentally disabled students. Then she nodded thoughtfully. "That is the real issue. We want people to take a close look at us. For the most part, they don't know anything about us."

"We could contact the newspaper reporters and let them interview some family members of our students," a man said thoughtfully. A secretary suggested finding ways to get more community people involved in the school's work.

Soon everyone was working together on an idea which blossomed over the next few months into what became an annual event, The Developmental Disabilities Awareness Fair. That first event included a white elephant silent auction, a melodrama presented in the auditorium (the actors were local politicians and community leaders), a fair complete with clowns, refreshments, games, and prizes, and a swap meet. A parade around the large campus included local bands and convertibles filled with sports figures, politicians, and local community leaders. Dozens of people from the community were actively involved in planning and running the event. Hundreds of people from the community attended the event, and over ten thousand dollars were raised for the school. The community became aware of the school, the students, and the realities of coping with a developmental disability.

All because someone made a "silly" suggestion that everyone in the community ought to spend some time at the school! What if the person who made that suggestion had been so shy or so afraid of rejection that the idea had never been voiced?

COMPARISON OF APPROACHES

Where you placed yourself on the pleasing continuum in the self-tests at the beginning of this book will give you a better idea of your usual approach to expressing your opinions.

The *Me Only* person voices an opinion whether or not anyone else wants to hear it. There is an expectation that others will not only listen to the opinion but also accept it and go along with it. Often the opinion carries with it a threat of reprisal if concurrence isn't forthcoming.

The *Me First* person is less demanding, but is unafraid to express opinions and to attempt to persuade others to go along. This person may listen to ideas of others, but only after his or her own ideas have been expressed.

The *We* person listens to others and voices opinions assertively and without apology, feeling free to disagree with the arguments of others.

The *You First* person waits to talk until everyone else has expressed ideas and opinions. Then, only after some coaxing will he share his.

The *You Only* person actively asks others to voice their opinions, but will not usually express his or her own opinions, except to concur with someone else.

Your Ideas Count

Everyone has ideas. I do. You do. And your ideas count. Some ideas are merely quick responses to a subject and are not based on facts, proof, or careful consideration. But because we all have different thinking patterns, even our quick responses can be helpful to a discussion. A linear thinker might get a good idea from a cluster thinker or a person whose creative associations seem disorganized. The linear thinker can add organization and tie up the details of a plan suggested by a dreamer.

The story of the feeding of the five thousand (John 6:1–14) tells of Andrew's response to a problem situation. He didn't know how to feed all of those people, but he did find a lad who had five loaves and two fishes. The idea of trying to feed the five thousand with that little amount of food was silly when viewed from a human perspective, but Andrew brought the boy to Jesus anyway. Those inconsequential loaves and fishes, combined with Jesus' miraculous power, were multiplied to feed the multitude. *Never underestimate the power of an idea.*

Some ideas we inherited, meaning that we grew up hearing them and along the way we started agreeing with or accepting them as our own. While a few of these might be better discarded, many of them are still around because we have found them to be valid and useful. Timothy was taught to have faith in God by his mother and his grandmother. His faith was strong because he "inherited" a lot of good, solid ideas (see Acts 16:1; 2 Tim. 1:5).

Many of your ideas are well thought out. You have read differing points of view. You have discussed the possibilities with friends. You have pondered both sides and made a considered judgment as to what you think about the issue. These are the ideas which let people know more about who you really are because so much of you has gone into the formulation of the opinion. Consider the story of Joshua and Caleb (Num. 13:26–14:38). They were two of the spies sent into Canaan before the Israelites crossed the Jordan. They surveyed the land, talked with the people, considered the alternatives, and believed that God would be faithful and lead them to victory. They were the only two who did. The others were fearful and were able to convince the tribes not to take the risk of entering the Promised Land.

Joshua and Caleb did their best. Their idea was unpopular, yet they were not afraid to stand up for their beliefs. And they were the only two of the spies who were eventually allowed to go into Canaan. The others perished in the wilderness.

Being willing to be open about our ideas, opinions, and thoughts is a step toward increasing the depth of our relationships. When we are open, we say we trust the relationship enough to take the risk. And there are risks.

THE RISKS OF BEING OPEN AND HONEST

There are several reasons people give for not being open and honest all of the time.

1. People don't want to make fools of themselves. Janine doesn't talk much because she is afraid she will say something foolish. She isn't confident in her ideas, even though she has learned that she has a great deal of good, common sense and can usually handle any situation with which she is faced. But because she doesn't have a good memory for facts, she is often unsure of just how valid her ideas are or how to back them up. So she just goes about her business quietly, doing what she thinks she needs to do.

If you are frequently afraid of saying something foolish, and you consequently keep quiet most of the time, it may be because you have decided that other people's opinions are better than your own. Take a look at your ideas. Are they impulsive? Or are they the result of careful consideration? Ask yourself why you believe that other people will think you are foolish if you have given the matter a lot of thought and come to a sound conclusion.

Try taking a few risks. In critical situations, do your homework. Gather the facts, write them down, and keep them handy for use in supporting your ideas and opinions. Practice voicing your opinions when your first impulse is to keep quiet. Try saying,

"I have an idea . . ."

"I think that . . ."

"I've always thought that . . ."

2. People don't want to reveal a lack of knowledge. Howard never learned about sports. He doesn't know the rules, doesn't follow the games, and feels very uncomfortable around other men when the conversation turns to sports. He tries to nod knowingly; if asked for a direct opinion, he says he hasn't quite made up his mind yet.

If you are afraid to let other people know that you have information gaps, you can take steps to fill in those gaps. You can take classes. Read books. Read the newspaper. Learn what you need to know to feel confident in your opinions. Ask questions and get other people to educate you as they share their opinions.

3. People don't want to argue. Marge will not discuss how she feels about the current foreign policy of the United States. She is deeply opposed to sending food to other countries when our own people go hungry. She hates that we are friendly with countries who oppress their people, and she doesn't agree with sending Americans to fight wars for other countries. But since a lot of her friends disagree with her, and since she doesn't want to argue, Marge has one rule: no discussion of the topic.

If you cannot stand conflict, debating, or disagreements, then you probably have adopted Marge's rule about some of the topics in your life. She knows what she thinks and believes, but she doesn't feel she needs to persuade others, and she certainly isn't about to be talked out of her opinions, so why discuss them?

There is some merit in drawing the lines and eliminating some of the unnecessary conflicts in your life, but if it becomes too much of a lifestyle, you are in danger of becoming very closed-minded. If you automatically shut down conversation about a topic once you have made up your mind on the subject, you are limiting the interactions you will have with friends, and your learning in that area will cease. You can listen and discuss a controversial topic without allowing the discussion to become a full-blown argument.

4. Sometimes people don't want to accept responsibility. The last time Phyllis spoke up at a committee meeting, she stated her idea of what could be done to improve the PTA. Immediately she was given the responsibility of implementing her idea. But she wasn't a good organizer or leader, and the good idea failed because the responsibility was given to the wrong person. Phyllis hasn't spoken out in a PTA meeting since.

If you have had a similar experience, you may have decided to keep your ideas to yourself, which may be a great shame because you probably have a lot of good ideas. One solution might be to share your idea privately with a friend and let him or her share the idea with the group. Another way would be to preface your idea with a disclaimer. "I am not the person to implement this idea, but I think that . . ."

5. *People don't want to be wrong.* Karen doesn't speak up right away because she doesn't ever want to be wrong. Karen would rather be thought to be shy, uninformed, shallow, and devoid of ideas than risk putting out an idea and having someone prove that her idea is wrong. She has a strong tendency to try to be perfect.

If you are so afraid of being wrong that you don't speak up, then you are probably telling yourself that to be wrong or misinformed is the same as being a personal failure. But you are struggling to meet unrealistic expectations because unless you have all of the facts—and incredible wisdom and insight—you are bound to be wrong in some of your ideas. We all are. We all have limited information, limited perspective, and a lack of total wisdom. We all are going to be wrong sometimes.

Everyone responds to these fears to some degree. No one wants to be considered foolish, uninformed, argumentative, or wrong; and no one wants the responsibility for implementing every idea every time. There are times when all of us would rather just be silent. The people pleaser, however, will have an exaggerated sense of these fears and will keep unusually quiet in those relationships in which he or she is a people pleaser.

PREPARE TO EXPRESS YOUR OPINIONS

As you decide to begin to speak up and express your ideas and thoughts, you might want to keep the following affirmations and guidelines in mind.

1. *God has not called you to a lifestyle of fearfulness.* "For God hath not given us the spirit of fear;

but of power, and of love, and of a sound mind" (2 Tim. 1:7).

This was a favorite verse of mine as I began to recover from my excessive people-pleasing behaviors. When I would begin to experience that familiar queasiness in my stomach and that shortness of breath, I would just remind myself that I didn't really have to be afraid. People pleasers live a life of fear which robs them of the freedom to speak up and let people know who they really are. Not only did God not intend for us live in fear, but He gave us power, love, and sound minds. Our ideas do count. We have value to Him. He created us with minds to think, to consider, and to draw conclusions. You have the right to your opinion.

2. *You have access to the power of the Holy Spirit in your thinking and in your reasoning.* "But the Comforter, which is the Holy Ghost, whom the Father will send in my name, he shall teach you all things, and bring all things to your remembrance, whatsoever I have said unto you" (John 14:26).

As you read, research, and consider matters, you have access to the power of the Holy Spirit to guide your thinking and assist you in making sound decisions, choices, and appropriate opinions.

3. *It is okay for you to have opinions which are different from those of others.* "I beseech you therefore, brethren, by the mercies of God, that ye present your bodies a living sacrifice, holy, acceptable unto God, which is your reasonable service. And be not conformed to this world: but be ye transformed by the renewing of your mind, that ye may prove what is that good, and acceptable, and perfect, will of God" (Rom. 12:1–2).

Sometimes your ideas will not conform to those of the world around you, particularly if you are viewing things from an eternal perspective. This is not to say that if your ideas are different, they are automatically right and the other person's are automatically wrong. Even Christians may in good conscience disagree with each other. Consider Paul and Barnabas's disagreeing over John Mark's suitability for a second missionary journey. It is not the end of the world when people don't agree.

When your listeners don't agree with you, don't start to back down in order to regain their approval. If sufficient information is presented to cause you to reconsider, you may choose to do so, but don't give up too easily on something you feel strongly about. Don't withdraw from the conversation just because someone has disagreed with you.

4. You don't have the right to force others to listen to your opinion if they don't want to. You can't *make* them agree with you. When Jesus sent out the twelve disciples on their own to teach and perform miracles, He gave them some guidelines. If people listened and accepted the disciples, they were to stay. But if people refused to listen and accept them, then the disciples were to shake the dust from their feet and depart from that city (Luke 9:1–6). We would do well to follow that same advice today.

When people are receptive to listening to your ideas then you are free to share. But if the reception is hostile and unproductive, you will gain little by continuing to argue your point.

5. Focus on expressing your ideas rather than on how people might respond. On the day of Pentecost, Peter and the disciples stood up in front of a crowd and began to preach about Jesus. They could be pretty sure that the reception would be mixed at best. What they were saying was unpopular and somewhat condemning, even though the final message was one of hope. Still, the disciples spoke out boldly. Peter's sermon as recorded in Acts 2:14–39 is articulate, clear, and compelling.

When you have something to say, it works best if you state it definitely, firmly, and convincingly.

I remember my first attempt to express my opinions or ideas. I was tentative and lacking in self-confidence. Don't do what I did. Don't start out with warnings or clarifiers such as,

"I could be wrong, but is it possible that . . ."

"I really don't know much about this, but I think that . . ."

"This is probably a stupid idea, but what about . . ."

Using such introductions merely sets the stage for your ideas to be immediately disregarded. You aren't giving the ideas value yourself, so why should others pay attention? A better approach would be to say,

"I think that . . ."

"What about . . ."

"Have we considered . . ."

When you know that you are going to express your opinions in a meeting or to a friend, you can plan in advance what you are going to say. Think through the best way to express what you want to say. Write it out. Rehearse by practicing. Say it aloud.

6. *Picture yourself being successful and articulate.* Mona sought my help in learning to express herself. I asked what she anticipated happening whenever she thought of voicing her ideas.

She responded quickly, "I'll say something stupid. People will laugh. I will be embarrassed." It was obviously a familiar mental image. And it was what kept Mona from being successful.

To help her overcome these feelings of inferiority, I had Mona create a new mental image. I told her to visualize herself as articulate, convincing, and self-confident with her audience listening respectfully. I asked Mona how she would feel if that mental image came true.

"I'd feel great!" Mona smiled.

You, like Mona, can choose which mental image will control your actions. She was letting a negative image prevent her from voicing her thoughts and ideas. Next time you want to say something, choose a successful mental image of yourself being articulate and persuasive to your attentive audience. If the fearful mental image comes into your mind, reject it. Substitute it with the new picture. *Change your picture and you can change your behavior.*

The first few times you speak up and express yourself in public, you may feel uncomfortable because you are doing something that is different from your normal pattern of behavior. Some people will be surprised. They are not used to your speaking out, and are not accustomed to having to consider your input. Some will support you by encouraging you to elaborate on one or more of your ideas. They will actively work to include you in future conversations and discussions.

Others will not respond positively. You may receive blank stares or outright negative reactions. A few people will attempt to discount your opinions, which is particularly painful when you are just learning to express yourself. Don't let a few negative responses shut you down. *Your opinions are valid and you have a right (sometimes even a responsibility) to share them.* Tell yourself that the negative responses you are receiving are simply the other person's opinion, which he or she has a right to express. If the response is overwhelmingly negative, consider the input. It may shed a new light on the subject and cause you to modify your opinion.

If you keep at it, you will become more skilled at expressing yourself. Your anxiety will go away, and you will no longer be afraid to join in discussions.

PRACTICE EXPRESSING IDEAS

The best way to become comfortable with a new behavior is to practice it in a safe setting. Each chapter in this book provides several suggestions for practicing the skills discussed. When you feel more comfortable with the new skills, start using them in real-life situations. This might mean practicing the skills with trusted friends who you know care for you and want you to grow. Even if your first attempts aren't successful, good friends can be supportive, particularly if you let them know you are learning a new behavior.

You can also practice your new skills in situations where you do not have a strong emotional involvement in the outcome. Rather than make your first attempt at publicly expressing your opinion at an important board meeting, choose a safer alternative. Speak up at an informal gathering of friends when they are discussing trivial matters.

Another way to practice is to think through and even write out what you would like to do or say in specific situations, and then rehearse aloud in front of a mirror or while driving alone. Having a thought is different from expressing it in words from your own mouth. Often we can *think* of the right things to say, but we can't get the words out. It takes practice.

Finally, for the most effective results, ask a friend to work with you to role-play situations in which you have difficulty expressing your opinion. Four practice scenarios are described below.

1. Your friend's station wagon is on its last legs and she asks you to help her pick out a new car. Your friend picks out a sporty red convertible, but you disagree with her choice. You feel the color shows dust too easily. You think that the leather seats

are impractical for someone with children. You think the payments are too high for her income. You think that the model is too "sporty" and not practical enough for a family car. How will you express your ideas to your friend?

2. There is a discussion at work about the new governor. Most of the people seem to like her. You disagree. The new governor has doubled the state budget, increased taxes, and requested that the legislature approve a $6 million redecoration project for the governor's mansion (which was repaired and remodeled five years ago). She has just announced layoffs of twelve thousand state employees in order to balance the new budget. How will you express your ideas about what she has done?

3. The school board has just announced that they are considering going to year-round sessions next year. You and your child don't like the idea. Your vacation plans will be messed up. Your child won't be able to go to church camp. Your child won't be able to have a summer job because there won't be a whole summer off, and you think that working summers is a good way for children to learn about earning money and taking responsibility. What would you say at the public hearing?

4. Your county is planning a new jail, and they want to put it in your neighborhood. You think this is a bad idea. You don't think that a jail ought to be near a school or a residential area. You are afraid for the safety of the community in case of an escape. You are sure property values will go down. What would you write to the planning commission about your viewpoints?

5

Confront Productively

Leanne and Gil are friends of mine. They had been married for six years before Leanne dared confront Gil about something that bothered her tremendously. Gil had this habit of flossing his teeth after every meal, regardless of where he was. Even in a restaurant, he would pull out his dental floss and floss between two teeth which always seemed to catch food. Leanne would die of embarrassment each time he did this. She would look away and try to pretend she was invisible. She tried making excuses for him by saying that food between his teeth hurt. She told herself that she ought to be grateful he wasn't at the other end of the continuum and didn't ever brush or floss his teeth. Nothing she told herself helped. She began to hate going out to dinner and made every excuse she could to avoid being with Gil in public when eating was involved. This began to seriously affect their social life. Finally, Leanne decided she had to say something.

When Leanne did confront Gil, he was surprised. After all, they had been married for six years. Why was this just being brought up? But he understood that while *he* saw nothing wrong with his behavior, Leanne was offended. So he agreed to excuse himself to the men's room after eating to floss his teeth.

The confrontation produced the desired results.

A Comparison of Approaches

Where you placed on the pleasing continuum in the self-tests at the beginning of this book will give you a good idea of your usual approach to confronting.

The *Me Only* person will confront anyone, anywhere, regardless of who is around and whether or not there would be a better time to confront. If this person is angry, everyone knows about it. If this person's rights are violated, reprisal is certain. This type of confrontation is seldom productive.

The *Me First* person will confront, but will usually be more gentle. After confronting, this person will listen to the "offender's" explanations.

The *We* person carefully chooses the time, place, and words to use in confronting. This person's goal is twofold—to resolve the problem and to save the relationship.

The *You First* person won't confront until confrontation is the only choice left, and then the confrontation is almost an apology for "bothering" the offender.

This person usually makes excuses for the offender so as to avoid confrontation as long as possible.

The *You Only* person gets sick, often literally, at the very idea of confronting. Fearing rejection, this person almost never confronts.

REASONS TO CONFRONT

There are times in almost any relationship when negative feelings exist. There are also times when these negative feelings may need to be expressed.

1. When you are justifiably annoyed or displeased. Carol's secretary, Fran, kept making personal telephone calls during work hours, even after Carol had explained the company policy of no personal calls. Carol had to confront Fran.

"As you are aware, our company policy is no personal calls," Carol told her. "I have noticed that you make a lot of unauthorized calls."

"But I have to check on my friend," Fran replied. "She's sick and might need me to stop by the grocery store on my way home."

"I'm sorry, but you'll just have to call from the pay phone on your break," Carol said firmly. "You cannot make personal calls during working hours."

"Okay," Fran sulked. But the calls stopped.

Ray's neighbor came into his garage again and "borrowed" the lawnmower without asking permission, even after Ray had already said he didn't want to loan it out any more. Ray needed to confront his neighbor.

"When you take my lawnmower without asking," Ray said, "I feel as if you don't care about our friendship. Actually, the lawnmower isn't working well and I cannot afford to buy a new one. I'm just hoping it will last a while longer. I really cannot afford to loan it out. Please don't take it again."

"Well, if you feel that way, I won't!" the friend said, a bit embarrassed and angry. A few seconds later the friend looked up and said, "I didn't understand. I'm sorry. I won't do it again."

One of the goals of confrontation is to resolve problems. In these two examples Carol and Ray had reason to be displeased with people who were not meeting their expectations—expectations that had been clearly stated. This may not always be true. In some cases you might, inadvertently, be part of the problem. If you have unrealistic expectations of others, you could think your "rights" are being violated when, in reality, you just need to revise your expectations. A confrontation may bring this to light and give you an opportunity to assist in the conflict resolution.

2. *When your basic rights are being violated.* In any relationship there are times when an individual yields personal rights and gives in to the desires of another. Sometimes this giving in is counterproductive.

At a seminar I gave not long ago, a lady named Rhonda told her story. She had walked up to the information counter in a store, waited her turn, and started to ask directions to the store in the chain which was participating in a special sale. She never got to finish her question. The response of the person behind the counter was totally inappropriate. Rhonda was subjected to a verbal attack. "If you people would only read the ad, you would know that this store is not participating in the special sale. Only the North End store is involved. I get so tired of unnecessary questions!"

Obviously, Rhonda didn't deserve the attack. A person assigned to work at an information counter is expected to give out information in a pleasant, polite manner. Because Rhonda decided to give in and not confront, she spent a futile two hours looking for the participating store. Not only did she miss out on the sale, but she also wasted valuable time driving around lost. She could have saved herself the time and frustration if she had just confronted the clerk and asked for directions.

Other situations where you do not want to avoid confrontation range from being shortchanged by a cashier or being given the wrong order in a restaurant to having decisions made for you and even to being abused in a relationship. If you are not receiving fair treatment from a public agency, if you are having difficulty returning defective merchandise, if people are talking loudly near you during a theater presentation, or if children are kicking the back of your airline seat— all these are situations where you should not shrink from confrontation.

As with anything, there must be a balance. You are not obligated to stand up for yourself every time you are wronged. It is up to you to choose whether or not you want to make an issue. The main concern is that you make a conscious choice and not allow others to make your choices for you. You may choose to turn the other cheek, to allow the other person to be rude without creating a confrontation, or to go the extra mile for someone who humanly speaking doesn't seem to deserve it (Matt. 5:38–46). The difference is that the people pleaser does this *without making a conscious choice*. He does it as a victim of habit rather than because he chooses to take that action in a particular situation.

Unresolved issues in relationships lead to disturbances in our relationship with God. Jesus told us to reconcile ourselves with our brother before we come to bring gifts to God (Matt. 5:23–24).

3. *When you want to know what someone is feeling*. While Carla was enthusiastically telling a group of friends at a party about the way she handled the latest problem situation with her children, she noticed Vern frowning at her. At first she thought there might

be something wrong with her appearance. A surreptitious peek in the mirror across the room assured her that she looked normal. She continued with her story for a little longer. Finally, she couldn't ignore Vern's frown any longer. She decided that he disagreed with how she had handled the situation. Her enthusiasm waned. A part of her felt angry. How dare he think he knew better than she did how to handle her own children? She turned on him and lashed out in anger.

"So, I suppose you think I handled that all wrong, just like you always do!" she nearly shouted at Vern. Then, with a shrug of her shoulders, she flounced out of the room.

If Carla had calmly confronted Vern instead of attacking him, she might have found out that he had a migraine headache and the light shining in his eyes increased the pain. He had barely been able to concentrate on Carla's story, let alone formulate an opinion about whether or not she had handled the situation well.

We are not mind readers. We do not know what is going on inside of someone else. Remember when the disciples rebuked the parents who brought their children to Jesus to be touched? Although they had lived with Him and been with Him on a daily basis since He began His ministry, the disciples had no idea what Jesus was thinking or feeling about those children. While "his disciples rebuked those that brought them," Jesus welcomed the children. He took them in His arms and blessed them (Mark 10:13–16).

4. *When you see someone doing something harmful.* Kurt walked into Geoff's garage and saw him operating his power saw in an unsafe manner. Worried that Geoff might seriously hurt himself, Kurt asked if he could point out a couple of things that would make the operation safer. Geoff agreed.

There are problems with confronting others when we see them doing something we consider wrong or harmful. If we aren't careful, we can begin imposing our standards on them, using our concern as an excuse to interfere in their lives. For example, Agnes considers it appropriate for her to confront any mother she sees in public who is not relating to her child in the way that Agnes considers to be right. Agnes is obnoxious about confronting!

Paul does write about confronting those who are doing wrong according to the Word of God. But, again, the confrontation is for the purpose of restoring the relationship, not for embarrassing others (1 Tim. 5:20; Gal. 6:1).

WHY PEOPLE DON'T CONFRONT

People pleasers develop many erroneous beliefs which keep them from being comfortable with confronting others.

1. Real friends don't get annoyed. Melinda, the daughter of a friend, won't confront her college roommate, who continually borrows her clothes. Melinda has convinced herself that if she were a true friend, she wouldn't care if her roommate borrowed the clothes. So Melinda often finds her things dirty when she wants to wear them.

Melinda's precept is wrong. True friends let friends know when something is bothering them so resentments don't build up.

2. If I can't say something nice, I don't say anything. Tina, a lady who goes to my church, never says anything negative about or to anyone. Of course, that doesn't mean Tina is always happy with things as they are. She simply stuffs her feelings. When the stuffing builds to overflowing and she finally resents someone enough, she breaks off the friendship and finds new friends, starting the cycle all over again.

Tina may run out of people to be friendly with unless she learns to confront.

3. I'd better leave it alone or I'll just get even more angry, and what would that solve? Stella isn't skilled at confronting, so the few times when she has spoken out about something, the conversations didn't go very well. In fact, the last time she confronted someone she made matters so much worse that she vowed never to speak up again.

Stella will have the same problem Melinda did. Unresolved problems don't go away, and they can sabotage a relationship.

4. People will think I am crazy or bad-tempered. Luke was once told he had a terrible temper and that he expected too much of people. He was five years old. He grew up trying to be extra-nice to overcome his "terrible" side. He is afraid to confront for fear someone will repeat the criticism.

Someone might. But is it really true? Probably not. Confrontation does not need to involve temper. Handled properly, it can be a very productive experience.

PREPARE TO CONFRONT

Properly handled confrontation does not happen automatically. There are many things involved, even before the confrontation occurs.

1. Be clear about why. Before confronting someone, you will want to be very clear about why you feel you need to confront that person. Ask yourself the tough question, "Why do I want to confront?" And answer it honestly.

The best reason to confront is because someone is doing something which is endangering your relationship with them, a relationship you value too much to allow yourself to become resentful. If what you want to point out is something that is not impacting your relationship, the answer to the question is very important. *Why do I feel it imperative that I step in and interfere? To prove that I am superior? To control someone? To be a Ms. / Mr. Fixit? To solve someone else's problems?* These are not good reasons!

2. *Decide when.* Confronting is a tough experience at best, so you should choose when to confront. If you know that when you are upset, ill, angry, or embarrassed, you don't handle situations well, do not confront then. Wait until you have had time to think through and sort out your feelings. Then consider carefully whether or not you were justified in your negative feelings. Once you are ready to discuss the issues rationally, seek out the other person and arrange for a time to talk.

3. *Plan the confrontation.* When planning the confrontation, be sure you take enough time to be fully prepared. You need to be able to describe how you were feeling (angry, frustrated, unloved, unappreciated, disappointed, or unhappy) and to identify what action triggered the negative feelings. You also need a clear view of what new actions you would like to see so the relationship can continue without hurts and resentments. Here are some examples:

> "Last night I felt unloved, unappreciated. You didn't show up for dinner and you didn't call and cancel. If you are not going to be able to keep our dates, please call me so I can make other plans."
>
> "I am very frightened when I ride in the car with you. I'm afraid we are going to have an accident. You drive very close to the cars in front of us. Would you consider not driving so close to other cars when I am in the car?"

Another important part of planning a confrontation is to assume responsibility for your own feelings.

In the examples above the speaker assumes responsibility for feelings and does not accuse the person being confronted of being responsible for those feelings. "I feel frightened" is better than "you frighten me." Words, labels, or accusations can trigger defensive responses. "You statements" such as those listed below guarantee a defensive response.

"You make me so angry."

"You don't love me!"

"You should be more careful!"

"You are a slob."

Assigning feelings or intentions to another person is nonproductive. Even if you think you know what the other person is feeling, or what he or she intended, ask questions rather than make accusations.

"You are quiet. What are you thinking?"

"You look puzzled. Am I making myself clear?"

"You are shaking your head. Do you disagree? In what ways?"

"Help me understand what happened. What were you thinking?"

Another point to remember is that if you have a problem, the other person does, too. And, in fact, you may be a part of the problem. I remember once when I had just received a promotion. The man who had held the position before me was transferred to another division. Two days later I heard from one of my staff that the man had called directly to the department head (who now worked for me) and stopped all activity in my department until a job he wanted done was completed. I was furious. How dare he think that he could run his new division, and mine as well? I carefully thought out what I wanted to say to him and how to say it so we could continue to work together. At first I couldn't think of how to approach the situation since I was clearly in the right and he was clearly in the wrong. But I valued his friendship, so I called and asked for a meeting.

When we got together I told him that I felt circumvented and undercut when he went around me and ordered my staff to stop everything I had told them to do until they did a job for him. I told him all he had to do was call me and I would take care of getting the job done. He thanked me, apologized, and then shared what had led up to that call. He had, indeed, contacted my office and spoken to my assistant. He had asked for assistance. She had told him she couldn't promise him any priority and that he could wait. He felt hurt. After all, he had been the division chief until two days before! Angry, he had reacted and called the department head who, loyal to the old boss, had responded.

Once again, I was reminded that whenever I am hurt, chances are the other person is hurt, too!

Remember to be gentle. Consider how you would respond if someone confronted you about the same thing in the way you plan to confront the other person. You might start a confrontation with words of gentle understanding:

"Perhaps you didn't mean to sound short, but when you responded to me that way, I felt attacked."

"You are basically a very nice person, but in this situation, I feel you aren't being fair and caring."

"I don't know if you realize it or not, but . . ."

When planning what to say, think of how you would respond to what you are saying. Practice aloud. Try different ways of saying the same thing. And remember to start off by stating that the reason you need to confront is that you value the relationship and this

problem *you both have* is hurting the relationship. Keep
it brief. Don't belabor the point to prove you are right.
Be ready to give examples if asked or to clarify your
feelings. Watch the tone of your voice. Be as calm and
relaxed as possible.

Then be prepared to listen. Invite feedback.
Ask the person to share his or her perception of the situation. You may end up being confronted as well.

4. Confront privately. Public confrontation is
so rarely appropriate that one could almost say, "Never
do it." When a person is confronted in front of others,
he or she is bound to feel embarrassed and, therefore,
unwilling to negotiate or work through a problem.

*5. After the confrontation, affirm the rela-
tionship.* Whatever the outcome of the confrontation,
whether or not the person agrees to do as you ask, you
need to affirm the value of the person and the value of
the relationship to you.

When I am in a situation in which I feel a need
to confront, I try to remember to plan the confrontation very carefully. I try to make sure that my attitude
is proper before I rush into the situation. I pray that
God will give me wisdom, gentleness, and the correct
words to get my message across. While confronting is
still not my most favorite activity, I have learned, after
years of practice, that if I do my part beforehand and
handle the situation carefully, the end result is usually so productive that it is worth the discomfort of the
confrontation.

Remember that productive confrontation is
not a *demand* that you get your way or that your rights
be respected. That kind of behavior is an aggressive
approach which violates the rights of others. Productive confrontation is a gentle presentation of how you
feel about a particular behavior on the part of someone
else, accompanied by a request for change. Your request
may be granted, or it may not. But you have been honest

with the other person, and that is the foundation for lasting relationships.

PRACTICE CONFRONTING

The best way to become comfortable with a new behavior is to practice it in a safe setting. Think of situations in which you are having difficulty confronting someone. Consider how you might appropriately confront. Write out what you would say. Then rehearse these situations aloud. Do it in front of a mirror or while driving alone or, better yet, ask a friend to role-play with you. When you feel more comfortable with the new skills, start using them in real-life situations.

If you can't think of situations from your own life, here are some to use for practice.

1. A client has cancelled three special meetings with you after you have rearranged your schedule to accommodate him. He wants to set up another meeting. (You might say, "I've already set aside three separate times for this meeting. I won't be able to reschedule again. I need to know if this is a firm commitment this time.")

2. You and a co-worker have been assigned a joint project, but you're doing all the work. (You might say, "This project was assigned to both of us. So far there hasn't been any input from you. Here's what I've done so far. What part can you work on?")

3. When a friend borrows your car it has a half a tank of gas. When the car is returned, it is so empty you run out of gas on the way to a gas station the next morning.

4. Your date is consistently late for the dinners you prepare for him or her.

5. A neighbor has borrowed your lawnmower from your tool shed without asking after you told him several times to please ask first.

6. A co-worker has been spreading rumors about you.

7. A friend is once more telling you how to run your life.

6

Ask for What You Want

I had a big problem. I decided to call my best friend and talk it over with her, but something held me back. Several times I reached for the telephone, but I couldn't bring myself to dial the number. Now I had a second problem! Why wouldn't, or couldn't, I call my friend? We had been confidants for over five years!

When I began to "analyze" my reaction, I realized that I was hesitant because I knew how my friend would respond. She would listen to my recital of the problem, and then immediately assume the responsibility for solving my problem. She would march off to confront the person I was having trouble with and would do my confronting for me. That wasn't what I wanted. What I needed was an empathetic listener, honest feedback, and friendly advice which I would be free to accept or reject. I didn't need someone to solve my problems for me.

I decided to work on my second problem first. I called my friend and asked her to meet me for lunch.

"I have a problem," I started out tentatively. "I really want to share it with you, but I find that I just can't do it!"

"Why not?" she asked, totally surprised.

"Because I really value our friendship and I want your input, but I don't want you to solve the problem for me. I don't want you to go talk with the other person. I don't want you to assume the responsibility for my problem. It is my responsibility."

"Well, that's just the way I am," she responded. "I can't stand it when my friends are being hurt or treated unfairly. I want to fix it."

"Would you try this time just to listen and discuss the problem with me to help me think clearly? Would you not get involved in trying to resolve the situation?"

"Well, I don't know if I can," she said honestly, "but I am willing to try."

I shared my problem, and together we discussed alternatives to resolving it. Then I resolved the problem on my own. In addition, my relationship with my friend was strengthened. My trust level was increased, and there could be increased intimacy. I no longer had to withhold my problems for fear that she would take over.

I could have decided not to ask my friend to give me what I wanted. I could have kept some doors closed in our relationship and found someone else with whom to discuss my problems. I could have said that I didn't trust the relationship enough to be honest and ask for what I really wanted from my friend. I'm glad I risked asking. Our relationship was strengthened. Confronting began a new and positive direction for our friendship, which has lasted over twenty years.

A COMPARISON OF APPROACHES

Where you fit on the pleasing continuum in the self-tests at the beginning of this book will give you a better idea of your usual approach to asking for what you want.

The *Me Only* person demands what he or she wants from everyone around.

Me First people don't hesitate to ask anyone for what they want. They expect to get what they want, but they start by asking nicely.

The *We* person not only asks for what he or she wants but also asks others what they want and seeks to work out either a give-and-take relationship or compromises.

You First people serve others, only asking for something when absolutely necessary—and then very hesitantly.

The *You Only* person rarely asks for anything, even if it something that is truly needed.

WHAT TO ASK FOR

Some people can ask for anything, and do. Others can ask for nothing and try to get through life completely on their own. The best choice lies between these two extremes. Some things are appropriate to ask for.

1. It is appropriate to ask for information when you need it, but not if you don't. Recently I met

Debbie, who had just been promoted to the personnel department of a large state agency. She had a good mind and learned quickly. Being task-oriented, she was soon outproducing other workers. She got documents processed on time and personnel problems resolved for employees. The rules governing civil service were complicated and filled two volumes, so when Debbie needed a quick check on one of the rules, she would turn to her supervisor, seated at the next desk, and ask her the question. Debbie was secretly irritated at the supervisor's consistent response, "Look it up."

Her supervisor knew that she wouldn't do Debbie any good to just tell her the information over and over. Debbie needed to learn to use her rule books and not to depend on the supervisor's presence to get her job done. Because the supervisor was wise enough to say no to Debbie's requests, Debbie became one of the best and most knowledgeable personnel workers.

A couple of desks away worked Oliver, another personnel technician. Oliver was the opposite of Debbie. He never asked for anything. If he didn't understand a rule, he just guessed at what it meant and processed the document. Many of his documents were returned with errors, and the employees, whose payroll checks were messed up month after month, were furious.

When information is needed, it is appropriate to ask whether it is for directions to a location, clarification of a rule or regulation, instructions on how to accomplish a task, confirmation of a conclusion after completing research, or amplification of someone's statements. When information can be researched for one's self, perhaps a little more work is needed before asking.

Asking for guidance and wisdom is a part of our relationship with God. James 1:5 tells us that, if we need wisdom, we are to ask of God and He will give it to us. We are told that the reason we don't have what we need is often because we don't ask (James 4:2).

2. *It is appropriate to ask for favors if you need them.* Kathy asks everyone for favors. In fact, when Kathy calls or comes over, the first thought people have is *What does she want?* Indiscriminately asking people to do things for her is a sign that Kathy feels she is only worthy or valuable when other people are serving her. She feels powerful when getting others to do things for her. She feels cherished if someone goes out of his way to help her. She is manipulative and passive-aggressive as she plays helpless to get favors, and yet becomes demanding or punishing if her requests are not granted.

In healthy give-and-take relationships, asking for favors is a normal interaction. Friends don't usually mind being asked to hand us a cup of coffee, pass the sugar, give us a ride to the airport, watch our children for an hour, help us with cleaning up the yard after a storm, or any number of other favors. This is especially true when they know that:

We would do the same for them if they asked.
They are free to say no to our requests.
We don't ask all of the time for everything.
We have done everything we could to help ourselves.

When Jairus's daughter was sick and he could do nothing to help her, he came to Jesus and asked a favor. He wanted Jesus to heal his daughter. Jesus agreed and went to Jairus's house and healed her (Mark 5:22–24, 35–42).

3. *It is appropriate to ask for assistance when you need it.* I'll never forget the day I tried to repair a leak in my waterbed all by myself. I wasn't about to ask one of my friends to give up a Saturday to help

me. I thought about it and finally conceived a plan which I thought would allow me to drain the waterbed, make the repairs, and refill the mattress. The plan made sense in theory, but not in practice. I got the mattress drained and the leak repaired, but when I tried to refill the mattress, I ran into problems. There I was, trying to refill the mattress with a hose charged with water when the hose slipped out of my hands. It was snaking around the bedroom, throwing water everywhere, while I desperately held the corner of the nearly-filled mattress so the water wouldn't run out of it. Neither the mattress nor the hose paid any attention to my screams of frustration. I was so angry that I became uncoordinated and took longer than necessary to cap the refill hole in the mattress. Then I ran outside to where the hose was hooked up, and turned off the water. In the minutes it took for me to do all of that, my bedroom was soaked. It took an hour to mop everything up, and the carpet was never the same afterwards. Since the mattress still needed additional water, I admitted that I needed help, went next door to a new neighbor I had never even met, and asked for assistance.

Some jobs just need more than one person. When we need assistance and won't ask for it, we are behaving foolishly. Many people pleasers are afraid to ask for assistance. They are afraid people will feel imposed upon or will help when they don't actually want to.

Appropriately asking for assistance does not mean putting off a task until you don't have time to get it done by yourself so you have to ask others to assist you. Peggy is like that. Because she doesn't budget her time well at work, when she has a large typing job she always ends up close to the deadline with insufficient time to finish. Then she asks everyone else in the office to assist her in meeting the deadline. This is an inappropriate type of request, especially when it occurs frequently.

It is appropriate, however, to ask for help when you need it. When Elijah was hungry and in need of food, God sent him to a widow to sustain him. When Elijah arrived, he asked the widow to make him some food. He had no way of feeding himself, and asked her assistance (1 Kings 17:8–16).

4. It is appropriate to ask for emotional support when you need it. William had a terrible day. As soon as he got home, he reached for the telephone and called his friend Barbara.

"I need a hug!" William admitted. "I don't want to eat dinner alone tonight, and I need to talk. Can you come over?"

"I'll be right there," Barbara said. "Want me to pick up some fried chicken on the way over? I promise a big hug and we can talk for hours."

We all need emotional support from time to time, and it is not unreasonable to ask someone for specifically what we need. We can't expect people to be mind readers. How many people are going to notice that we are more quiet than usual today and give us tea and sympathy? If we need a little emotional space because we are stressed out, we can ask that people not make demands on us for a day or so. If we need a listener, we can ask. If we need to be distracted from a worrisome problem, we can ask a friend to join us for an afternoon of fun. If we need prayer, we can ask our friends for support.

When Jesus was facing His darkest moment, He took three of His closest disciples into the Garden of Gethsemane. He shared His innermost feelings with them. He said that His soul was exceedingly sorrowful. He asked them to watch with Him as He went to pray. But when He came back, He found them asleep. So He woke them and asked them again to watch and pray with Him. Even the Son of God asked for emotional and spiritual support when He needed it from His friends (Matt. 26:36–46).

Yet it is important to note that, when the disciples couldn't provide the support Jesus asked for (they kept falling asleep), He did not attack them after the second request. He accepted the fact that they were unable to meet His request. We should keep in mind that the people we ask to do something for us may not be able to meet that need. We may have to ask someone else.

Sometimes our real comfort comes from God rather than other people (2 Cor. 1:3–5). But it is still nice to feel human arms around us giving us a much-needed hug when life has trampled us down and we are emotionally bruised and bleeding.

5. It is appropriate to ask for attention. Sam's wife is a busy lady. She works full-time, takes care of household duties, is active in the PTA, sings in the church choir, teaches a home Bible study group one evening a week, and is taking a college class in gourmet cooking. Most of what she does benefits the family, but Sam sometimes feels as if his wife is never there for him. Even when they are together, it seems that her mind is somewhere else planning her next task. Finally, Sam talked to his wife.

"I really feel a need for some of your attention. I'd like for us to set aside one evening a week as a time we can be together and really focus on each other. We can stay home, go out to dinner, go for a walk, or work on a project. But I want to talk. I want you to share with me what you are thinking, planning, struggling with, and feeling. I want to be a part of your life, but I don't feel genuinely connected with you these days. I need some attention."

Sam's wife agreed. Getting into a new routine was not always easy, and sometimes a couple of weeks would go by without Sam and his wife having their night together. But things began to improve, and soon they were both looking forward to their evening together. Their relationship deepened and improved.

Although we should feel free to ask for emotional support when we need it, people pleasers often use that as a substitute for approval. They feel valued only when someone is giving them attention. It is not appropriate to ask for excessive attention. We cannot be the center of attention at every gathering and in every relationship.

6. *It is appropriate to ask for permission to do something your way.* Richard and Donna were disagreeing about the best way to approach a specific problem. After a lengthy discussion, they were no closer to a solution than before. Finally, Richard asked for what he wanted. "I really want to try it this way. If it doesn't work, then we'll try your way, okay?" Donna agreed.

When there is no possibility of coming to an agreement and a compromise is unrealistic, it is okay to ask for what you want.

When Daniel was brought to the king's court and given royal food from the palace, Daniel knew that the food was not proper for him to eat as a Jew. So he asked the prince of the eunuchs to assist him in obtaining permission to eat proper Jewish food (Dan. 1:6–15). Daniel needed help to achieve what he purposed in his heart—not to defile himself with improper foods. He needed permission to try things his way. He was granted that request, and God blessed him for his faithfulness.

When we come to God to ask for what we need from Him, Matthew tells us to be sure and ask, believing that we will receive (Matt. 21:22).

WHY WE DON'T ASK

So why don't we ask for what we need? Often the answer to that question involves one or more of the following false beliefs:

- Asking is imposing. If I ask someone for something, he or she will feel obligated to me. I don't want people doing things for me they don't really want to do.

- Asking makes me vulnerable. If I ask and someone says no, I feel rejected.

- No one would want to help me.

- Asking for things leaves me obligated to give back if the other person asks me next time.

- People should know what I need or want without my having to ask all of the time.

These beliefs are based on a poor self-esteem and a lack of understanding about healthy relationships. Perhaps people holding these beliefs have had bad experiences with asking for what they want. Perhaps they didn't get what they wanted. Perhaps others threw their requests in their faces or used rejection as a weapon of deliberate hurt.

PREPARE TO ASK

Whether you are just beginning to make requests in relationships or are already successful in asking for what you need, there are guidelines to consider.

1. Make sure your request is reasonable. Often we don't get what we ask for because we are being unreasonable. We don't intend to be unreasonable, we just may not have thought through what we are requesting.

When I was single, I dated one man who was often late for our dates. At times I would work hard to prepare a delicious meal, only to wait . . . and wait . . .

and wait. He didn't even call to say he wasn't coming. I was angry and hurt. I knew that if he really cared about me, he would call. Finally I got up enough courage to ask him to call me whenever he wasn't going to come or when he was going to be late. After all, I couldn't afford to keep wasting food by cooking it for him, only to have him not even show up. I thought I was being incredibly reasonable in asking for a telephone call when what I really wanted to do was scream at him and throw the ruined food in his face!

Then he reminded me that there was another side—his. He was a labor negotiator and was in the middle of negotiating master contracts with several large companies. A session scheduled for an hour or two in the afternoon could go on all night without warning. Food would be ordered in and no one would leave the bargaining tables except to go to the restroom. He wasn't free to make telephone calls or to keep our dates on such occasions. My "reasonable" request turned out to be "unreasonable."

We compromised. He asked that I not prepare food until he arrived, even if that meant we would eat a little later. That way, I wouldn't be wasting food.

One way to see if your request is reasonable is to ask the other person if he or she believes it to be unreasonable. Listen to the other person's interpretation of your request. It may be that you won't agree on what is reasonable, and you will have to make decisions about whether or not you are going to keep asking—and whether or not you are going to pursue the relationship if the request is a critical one for you.

Hilda thought it was reasonable for her to ask Jason not to date other women after they became engaged. Jason didn't think it was a reasonable request because they weren't married yet. To Hilda this was a red flag, and she wisely decided to break the engagement.

2. Make sure your request is clear. When Sam asked his wife for attention, he didn't just say, "I'd like you to give me more attention." He outlined exactly what he wanted: one night a week set aside for the two of them for interaction and sharing.

When your requests are not specific and clear, you probably won't get what you want. Don't say, "I'd like you to be more thoughtful." That is not a specific request. Instead, say, "I'd like you not to drop your clothes all over the bedroom, especially when I've just spent all day cleaning up the house." Rather than telling your spouse, "Please don't be such a tightwad," say, "When we go out to dinner, I'd like you to tip at least 15 percent."

3. Ask the right person. If you want someone to go shopping with you, be sure you ask a person who enjoys shopping. Don't ask a friend who thinks shopping is a bore, a chore, or a drudgery. Neither of you will enjoy the day. If you need a favor, ask someone who can grant the favor. If you need information, ask someone who knows what you want or need. If you want assistance, ask someone who can provide that assistance.

These guidelines seem simple, but we often aren't discriminating when choosing people to do something for us, and then we get angry at them for not being able to grant our request. For instance, when Harriet's drier broke, she asked her friend Max to come take a look at it. He did and then gave his considered opinion, "It's broke!" Max didn't know any more about how to repair the dryer than Harriet did, but Harriet didn't care. She was upset that Max wouldn't solve her problem. Max was the wrong person to ask!

4. Ask, don't demand. The key to successful asking is not to demand, but to request. No one has a right to demand things of others. All we can do is ask for what we want and see if the other person will or can give us what we need.

Say, for example, "Would you be willing to drive the kids to their soccer game this Saturday?" or, "Would you try to not tell those kinds of jokes in front of me?" or, "I need some help with the household chores in the evenings. Would you rather take out the trash or clean up the kitchen?" No guilt trips. No reminders about who "sacrificed" last time. No threats.

5. *Allow the other person to say no without reprisal or your feeling rejected.* Understand that people will respond differently to your reasonable requests. Some will grant the request; others will overreact because of their own past experiences. Some will refuse. Some will accuse you of being demanding even when your request is gentle and phrased as a request.

6. *Time your requests properly.* Asking people to do something for you when they are overloaded, stressed out, angry, upset, ill, or busy may result in your requests being denied. When possible, time your requests so that they have the greatest chance of being granted.

Louise called a friend for some information she needed on the procedure for filing for a teaching credential. When her friend answered the telephone, Louise heard a lot of tension in her voice.

"Would it be better for you if I called back later?" Louise asked.

"Please," the friend responded gratefully. "The baby is crying and I'm in the middle of trying to get the kids settled down for the night."

Louise might have incorrectly interpreted the tension in her friend's voice as unwillingness to help her and been offended. Instead, she understood that sometimes the timing of requests is critical.

7. *Don't ask just to be asking.* Only ask when you need to ask. Don't play "baby" and ask for everything all of the time. People get tired of those who act helpless and who won't help themselves.

8. Don't ask if you don't want what you ask for. Jill called a friend and asked her to go to a movie with her. The friend had other plans and said she couldn't go. When Jill expressed disappointment, the friend said she would try and cancel the other plans. However, when the friend called back fifteen minutes later, having successfully changed her plans, Jill had reconsidered and no longer wanted to go to the movies. Not a good move, Jill.

When you learn to follow these guidelines, your requests will be gentle, accepting, clear, reasonable—and usually granted if you ask the right persons. At first the risk of asking will feel uncomfortable because it is an unfamiliar experience. But with practice, you will become more at ease.

Some people pleasers just can't ask anyone for anything. They can't ask others to be quiet in a movie or church service. In the grocery store they won't ask to go ahead of someone with a cart full even if they only have one item and are paying cash. Yet these are simple and reasonable requests. One problem is that people pleasers don't have the power to ensure that others will comply with their requests, so they are afraid of being rejected if they ask. A people pleaser will often suffer in silence rather than ask for something.

PRACTICE ASKING FOR WHAT YOU WANT

As discussed in chapter 4, the best way to get comfortable with a new behavior is to practice it in a safe setting. You can probably think of many situations where you would have difficulty asking for what you want. Once you have determined that a situation is an appropriate one for asking and you have planned and written out what you would say, you need to rehearse the situation aloud. Good places to rehearse include in front of a mirror or while driving alone. One of the best is role-playing with a friend. Once you feel more comfortable with the new skills, you can start using them in real-life situations.

If you can't think of situations from your own life, here are some to use for practice.

1. You are planning a surprise party for your spouse and need to know how to make a cake. Ask for information.

2. You are leaving town and you need someone to take care of your dog. Ask for a favor.

3. You are building the set for a community play. You need assistance from a friend. Ask for help. (Remember to be specific. You might say, "Would you be willing to assist me this Saturday afternoon for four hours building the set for the community play?")

4. You have had a bad day at work. Ask a friend for a hug.

5. Someone you care about very much doesn't give you the attention you feel you want from this relationship. Ask for what you want. (You might say, "I'd like to spend more time alone with you instead of always sharing you with your friends. Could we spend next Sunday afternoon alone together from 2:00 until 5:00?")

6. You and a friend are disagreeing about the best way to pack the trunk of the car for a joint trip. Ask for permission to pack it your way.

7. You are struggling with a problem with your boss at work. You need wisdom about how to deal with the situation. Ask a friend to pray for you.

7

Refuse Unreasonable Requests

It had been a long week at work. Several rush jobs had been completed, even though two of the other secretaries had been out sick. The unusually hot and close weather had seemed to create a bit of tension in the office. Irene was anxiously looking forward to the weekend. She had been planning this trip all week. At five o'clock on the dot she was going to rush home, make a quick change of clothes, pick up her already-packed suitcase, and drive to the mountains. As she closed her eyes she imagined that she could already smell the pines. Less than one hour and she could leave!

As a co-worker approached her desk, Irene's heart sank. She could tell what was coming. She was right.

"Irene," her co-worker said, "I need you to help me by sending out these letters. It won't take you but a couple of hours or so, and you could use the overtime. I have plans for the weekend, so I can't stay. I gotta run!" The co-worker dropped the letters on Irene's desk and turned without waiting for her answer. She already knew what Irene would say. She was right.

"Sure. No problem," Irene automatically responded. It wasn't the first time that her co-workers asked Irene to help them with their work. Looking at the pile of letters, she could tell she would be there at least three more hours. "Oh well," she sighed. "I'll just drive to the mountains in the morning." Sighing, she picked up the first letter and began.

Irene has a problem with setting limits in her relationships. She can't seem to say no even when the requests are obviously unreasonable.

A Comparison of Approaches

Where you placed on the pleasing continuum in the self-tests at the beginning of this book will give you a better idea of your usual approach to unreasonable requests.

The *Me Only* person responds with an incredulous, "You've got to be kidding!" or an attack, "You've got your nerve asking me to do that!"

The *Me First* person rarely says yes to an unreasonable request. The denial is usually gentle, but firm. "I can't do that; I have other plans."

The *We* person listens to requests, considers the wants or needs of the other person as well as his or her own needs, and, when possible, works out a workable compromise. "I can't help you this time, but if you ask me earlier next time, I will see what I can do." Or, "I have plans this weekend, too, but if we both stay for an hour I'll bet we can get these letters out."

The *You First* person might attempt to set a limit for the future, but would not refuse the request. "Okay this time, but next time please ask someone else."

The *You Only* person says yes to the request, whatever it may be. This person sacrifices personal plans, time, and desires in order to comply with the wishes of others.

LIMITS ARE NECESSARY

Even as she typed the letters, Irene knew that once again she had failed to take care of her own needs. She had let her co-worker take advantage of her one more time. Limits are necessary in relationships. The following are some reasons why.

1. Without limits, you spread yourself too thin. Nicole can't say no. Everyone knows it. In fact, friends even joke about it. Whenever there is an unpleasant task, someone will say, "Ask Nicole—she can't say no!" And someone usually does. As a result, Nicole rarely has a minute to herself or time to do what she wants to do. She is too busy doing things for everyone else.

Almost every night of the week, Nicole is booked. There is a Bible study in her home on Mondays, and she is team scorekeeper for the bowling league on Tuesdays (she personally doesn't like to bowl). On Wednesdays she works with the girls' group at church, then attends choir practice. On Thursdays she babysits for a neighbor, a single parent who is attending college and can't afford to hire a sitter. On Fridays she sets up the room, makes coffee, and acts as greeter at the singles' group at church. Saturdays she does her chores, but usually is also running errands for friends and neighbors. Frequently on Saturday night she bakes cookies or cupcakes for Sunday school (the fellowship chairman knows that if no one else will do it, Nicole will not say no). On Sundays Nicole doesn't have any set plans, but people usually fill her day with various requests.

If someone needs an errand run, a garage cleaned, a bookcase delivered, a child watched, a cake baked, or a drain unclogged, Nicole gets the call. Nicole is spread so thin, she is emotionally drained. Even though she knows it would be healthy for her to have some time alone, some time to do her own things, Nicole can't make herself say no. And although her "okay" sounds pleasant enough, resentment is slowly building inside her. She is tired. She knows that everyone is taking advantage of her. She can't meet all of the requests, no matter how hard she tries. Sooner or later she lets someone down and they get angry with her. The irony is that she doesn't say no because she doesn't want to be rejected, but by saying yes to everything she overloads herself to the point that she ends up being rejected anyway because she can't do it all, all of the time.

If you can't say no, you will become involved in situations you will later regret. You may have wasted your time, linked up with someone you do not particularly like, or committed to doing something you actually hate to do.

2. *Without limits, the requests will just keep coming.* Until Nicole and Irene learn to say no, people will continue to make unreasonable requests. By being silent, people pleasers give permission for the requests to continue. Even when the askers know they are being unreasonable, they ask anyway because they are sure the people pleaser will not refuse their request. The only way to keep others from taking advantage of

you and to keep them from making unreasonable requests, is to set appropriate limits for yourself.

Without limits, you will become a martyr, sacrificing yourself and your freedom for others. Some people pleasers might consider it worthwhile to spend their lives sacrificing for others—if it guarantees the eternal approval they so desire. But even after years of saying yes, the people pleaser is still subject to rejection or disapproval the first time he or she decides to say no. No matter how many unreasonable requests you say yes to, it will never be enough for those who want to take advantage of you. You will come to feel used, abused, and manipulated, finding yourself doing things you wish you didn't have to do.

3. *Without limits, you won't have a life of your own.* As Nicole knows, her life or her time isn't her own. When she wants to rest, she often finds herself rushing around doing things for other people. When she is craving a pizza, she may eat Mexican food because that's what someone else wants.

One night, just before Christmas, Nicole was sitting on the floor in the middle of her living room wrapping Christmas presents for a friend. The friend was at a party and asked Nicole to wrap her presents because she didn't have time. As Nicole looked around at the pretty packages of wrapped packages, she realized that her own presents were still unwrapped in the closet. She suddenly thought of her "too-busy" friend enjoying herself at a party. Nicole realized that she wasn't at the party—and she wasn't getting her own gifts wrapped. She decided that there was something wrong and determined to begin making some changes. She decided to stop and not wrap the rest of her friend's packages.

4. *Without limits, you may become untruthful.* Because Nicole had agreed to wrap the packages, and because she didn't want to risk disapproval, she

wasn't exactly truthful when her friend showed up after the party to collect the packages. Nicole left the wrapping paper strewn around the room, and sat in the middle of the packages as if she had been working all evening.

"I did as many as I could before you got home," Nicole told her friend sadly, "but I just couldn't finish!"

In the next few days, determined to not give in to unreasonable requests, Nicole found herself actually lying to keep from saying a straight-out no. She said she was exhausted, sick to her stomach, coming down with a cold, already committed to doing three other things, and even that she was allergic when a friend asked her to petsit her cat! Because she was unable to set reasonable limits for herself, Nicole became dishonest.

Actually, Nicole had been just as untruthful before. She hadn't been honest when she always said yes and acted as if she were glad to be doing all of those things for others. Not setting limits caused Nicole to be dishonest in her relationships.

5. Without limits, your relationships suffer. Years ago I took my two sons for an extended trip to a favorite vacation spot. We had scrimped and saved for the trip, and had found an incredibly inexpensive motel room with a tiny kitchenette. If we were careful, we could afford to stay for five weeks.

I was telling a group of friends and acquaintances about the deal when one lady spoke up, "I have some vacation time coming up, too. Why don't I come over and join you?"

"Sure," I said, trying not to let my dismay show in my voice. I didn't even know this lady very well, and all I could hope was that she wouldn't follow through on her impulsive idea. What I really wanted was time alone with my sons—time to rest and read books and time to take walks by myself in the woods.

But I didn't know how to tell this lady what I wanted or how to tell her that her request to join us was not okay with me.

Despite my desperate hopes to the contrary, she joined us for the last week of our vacation. She shared our tiny room, and had a miserable time. We had already done the "tourist" things the first four weeks we were there. We had developed a routine which suited us. We were ready to just vegetate for the last week, reading, swimming, and soaking up the last few days of the wonderful sunshine before going home. She was ready to go sightseeing and have some action-packed fun. I think we were all glad when Friday came and it was time to go home.

Even though that lady was a super person, she and I never became any more than acquaintances. I think it was because I had not been honest with her, and as a consequence her vacation was disappointing for her. Her visions of the fun we would have never came true. My vacation wasn't as peaceful as I had hoped it would be. Both of us suffered because I wasn't honest enough to tell her no in the beginning. Saying no isn't easy for a people pleaser.

It is interesting to me that most of us learn early in life to say no adamantly and with great emotion. During the "terrible twos," the word no is usually a favorite as young children try to set all kinds of limits in their lives. But somewhere along the way, the ability to say no gets trained out of those of us who grow up to be people pleasers. We get used to giving in to the requests of others. We may have been taught to do that by our parents. We may have discovered that when we say yes we get temporary approval from others. We may have had good experiences when we have said yes. We may actually be afraid to say no. People pleasers equate saying no with not pleasing others. They feel scared or guilty if they ever put their own needs first.

They don't value themselves enough to give priority to the things they want and need.

IT'S HARD TO SAY NO

Why is it hard to say no? Often it's because we have developed a set of beliefs that it isn't appropriate to say no. Some of the beliefs are discussed below.

1. If it's a worthy cause, I should say yes. How does one go about saying no when the cause is worthy? People pleasers get involved in door-to-door solicitations for charities, sewing projects for orphanages, collecting toys for homeless children, knitting slippers for senior citizens, teaching adult literacy classes, painting the church, and a hundred other good causes. But regardless of how many good causes you help, there are always going to be more out there. I am reminded of Jesus' response to Judas, who criticized Mary's pouring of ointment on Jesus' feet as a costly waste. Judas thought that the ointment ought to have been sold and the money given to the poor. Jesus rebuked him, saying that the poor would always be with us (Matt. 26:6–13). There will always be good causes with us, no matter how many we say yes to. We have the right to set priorities and to set appropriate limits.

2. I owe it to someone to say yes. My friend Marlene went shopping. She tried on at least twenty dresses, but found nothing she really liked. Yet when the salesperson pressed her to buy, Marlene felt guilty for having taken up so much of the woman's time that she bought not one, but two of the dresses. Marlene felt she owed the saleswoman for the time she spent, so she said yes.

So did Lloyd. Ginny had invited him over for a home-cooked meal. She had mended his jacket for him. She had spent three hours listening to his problems about work. Then she asked him to spend the night. He didn't want to, but he did. He didn't know how to stand up for his ideals and say no.

People pleasers often see saying yes as a payment for taking up the time or energy of another person. Saying yes is not the only alternative. There are plenty of other ways to repay others if necessary.

3. Friends do not say no. Suzanne told me the other day that she simply doesn't say no because she firmly believes that genuine friends do not refuse requests. Her expectation of herself is unrealistic. She does notice that some of her friends—most of them, in fact—do sometimes say no to her, but she finds excuses for their behavior rather than recognizing that she also has the right to say no.

The disciples James and John were close friends of Jesus. One day they came to Jesus and asked if He would promise them that in glory they would sit on either side of Him. Jesus, even though He was their friend, said no to their request (Mark 10:35–40). Friends are allowed to say no, especially when requests are unreasonable or unfair.

4. It is easier to live with myself if I say yes. Letty has so trained herself to say yes that if she ever must say no, even with an irrefutable excuse, she feels bad. She will go out of her way to make it up to the person over and over until some of her guilt goes away. For her, it is easier to just say yes and do whatever is asked, no matter how unreasonable it may be or how she may feel at the time.

Letty needs to study how Jesus sometimes said no. He had what the multitudes needed: wisdom, love, teachings, healing power, and even food. Yet sometimes when the crowd became too much, Jesus said "no more" and went away with His disciples. He knew the value of setting limits on His time and energies, even when He was desperately needed by the people (Matt. 15:39; Mark 4:35–36). Sometimes Jesus even left His disciples and made time for Himself to be alone (Matt. 14:23).

Learning to say no means being able to abandon beliefs which are nonproductive and unrealistic.

PREPARE TO SAY NO

You will need to prepare carefully if you are going to change your people-pleasing behaviors. Actually, learning to say no is one of the hardest people-pleasing habits to let go of. Have a piece of paper and a pen or pencil handy as you go over the following steps.

1. Take a look at your life. Where are you having the most difficulty saying no? To everybody? To your boss? To your friends? To your children? To your partner? To persons in authority?

In what situations do you find yourself saying yes when you really want to say no? Requests for your time? Money? Energy? Home? Things?

What is this costing you? What are you giving up because you can't say no? Make this list as long as you can, for it is the basis you will use to keep yourself on track once you start on the road to saying no.

Listen carefully to each request. Ask for clarification if you are unsure just what you are being asked to do. You may want to take time to make a decision about whether you choose to say yes or no.

2. List ways to say no kindly but firmly. You don't want to turn your no into an attack. Remember, the other person has a right to ask for what is wanted. And you have a right to determine if the request is reasonable for you. The purpose is not to make the asker feel guilty for having asked, but to set limits in your own life.

You might respond by saying, "I have other plans for Saturday" or, "I can't take on any new projects right now" or, "I won't be able to help you out this time." If people aren't used to hearing you say no, you may have to repeat your refusal a couple of times before they really believe that you mean it.

3. Don't apologize for saying no. There is no need to apologize for not saying yes all the time. Nor do you need to make it up to people to whom you say no. And don't give long explanations or justifications about why you are saying no.

Don't say things like:

"I am really sorry. I have already made plans. If I could change them, I would."

"If there were any way I could, I would do it."

"I really wish I could say yes, but I can't."

Such statements might be interpreted as tentativeness on your part, and an opportunity to talk you into saying yes. People might find a flaw in your logic or the weakness in your decision and attempt to manipulate you into changing your mind.

4. Don't lie about why you are saying no. You don't have to explain at length that you are learning to set limits in your life and that you must refuse unreasonable requests, but you don't want to lie about why you are saying no. A simple, "No, I can't do that for you" is more than sufficient. Don't pretend to be ill, committed elsewhere, or that your spouse won't let you. Just say no.

5. Be prepared for a negative response. The responses to your no may range from a shrug of the shoulders and an, "oh, well," to outright indignation. You will want to be sure not to give in and retract your no just because you have disappointed someone. Be prepared for your no to disappoint someone. The person who asked wants something from you, even if it is an unreasonable request, and you are not giving what is wanted.

Learning to set limits in your life will create a new level of honesty in your relationships. I have a friend who is not very good about setting limits in her relationships. I am often afraid to ask her for anything for fear she will say yes when she ought to say no. I feel as if I must always check and recheck with her to be sure that her yes is really okay.

I have another friend who is very good about setting limits. When I ask for something, I am confident that if she says yes it is because she wants to. If she doesn't want to, or finds the request unreasonable, she will say no. It is wonderful not to have to worry about whether or not her yes is really okay. To tell the truth, I much prefer dealing with this friend. She takes care of herself so I don't have to.

Set appropriate limits. Say yes when it is appropriate and something you really want to do. And learn how to say no when the request is inappropriate or something you do not want to do. Learn to take care of yourself.

PRACTICE SAYING NO TO UNREASONABLE REQUESTS

The best way to get comfortable with a new behavior is to practice it in a safe setting. Think of situations in which you are having difficulty saying no to unreasonable requests. Write out what you would say. Rehearse aloud these situations in front of a mirror or while driving alone. Better yet, ask a friend to role-play with you. When you feel more comfortable with the new skills, start using them in real-life situations.

If you can't think of situations from your own life, here are some to use for practice.

1. A person at work keeps borrowing small change and doesn't ever pay it back. Now he wants to borrow 75 cents. (You might say, "No. I have decided that I won't lend you any more money until you have paid back what you have already borrowed.")

2. You and a friend are having a quiet dinner together when other friends drop by and want to join you. (You might say, "It's great to see you, but we've planned a special evening. Perhaps we could get together another time.")

3. There is a persistent door-to-door salesman who wants you to buy a vacuum cleaner. You are trying to watch your budget and definitely don't need his product.

4. A neighbor wants you to babysit for free for the third time this week.

Part III

Reach Out— Become More Caring

8

Initiate Contact

Cynthia took one last look in the long mirror in her hotel room. Her smart, black-and-white suit was perfect: businesslike with a touch of understated elegance. Her dark hair was arranged in a flattering style which brought out the sparkle in her big, brown eyes. She thought, *There is nothing left to do except to go down to the reception and mingle*. The thought made her slightly queasy.

Cynthia had been chosen as a representative from her company to the business convention of the year. All the important people in the industry would be there. She looked forward to the seminars because she would hear all of the latest developments in her field, and by taking copious notes, she would be able to bring back the information to her boss. The trade show was a must-do. She couldn't wait to wander down the aisles, checking out the most modern equipment and picking up literature which would keep the company on the competitive edge of the industry. What she felt uneasy about were the in-between times, the informal gatherings during which she would be expected to mingle and talk one-on-one with other attendees.

Cynthia was intelligent, capable, and quite knowledgeable in her industry. But she just wasn't comfortable initiating contact with people. She was shy. She was afraid. She was unskilled in making small talk. The reception was her biggest fear.

A COMPARISON OF APPROACHES

Where you placed on the pleasing continuum in the self-tests at the beginning of this book will give you a better idea of your usual approach to initiating contact.

The *Me Only* person walks up to anyone, anywhere, and initiates contact without even considering if he or she is interrupting another conversation. There is no hesitation or fear that the interruption may not be welcome.

The *Me First* person is unafraid of making contact and will approach anyone, but he or she will be polite about interrupting a conversation, and will wait until there is a lull in the conversation.

The *We* person sometimes makes the initial contact and sometimes waits for others to make the contact. If the *We* person wishes to make contact with someone engaged in another conversation, he or she will either wait until the conversation is over or will ask permission to join the conversation. The *We* person may simply let the other person know that contact is desired and leave the time and place up to the other person.

The *You First* person may look longingly at someone with whom he or she desires contact or may attempt to "accidently" bump into the other person, but won't usually initiate the contact unless there is a compelling reason to do so.

The *You Only* person is so afraid of imposing that contact is seldom initiated. This person is a responder only, and then he or she is often secretly convinced that the other person doesn't really want the contact. Any contact or interaction by others is interpreted to be out of pity, necessity, or because something is needed to be done. It never occurs to a *You Only* person that anyone would just want to talk to him or her.

RESPONDERS MAY MISS OUT

When Cynthia finally made herself walk into the dreaded reception, she looked around a bit like a frightened rabbit in a room full of hunters. But she forced a smile and tried to mingle. Holding tightly to her cup of coffee, she moved around the room, never stopping to initiate contact, never giving eye contact, and never responding with more than one or two words to attempted contacts from others. She was miserable.

After forty-five minutes she felt as if she could not stand a minute more. *Why stay?* she asked herself. *I'm not making any contacts.* Convinced that it made sense to leave, Cynthia left the room through the nearest door. It led to a small porch outside of the reception room. The porch was deserted except for a man Cynthia immediately recognized as one of the foremost leaders in the industry. His ideas were revolutionary and his insights and vision were the wave of the future. Cynthia was one of his biggest admirers. She had often thought of how great it would be to meet this man and discuss some of his ideas that had impacted her greatly. Now here he was, all alone, looking out over the city lights as if enjoying the view.

Cynthia turned and bolted back into the reception room, found another door, and made her exit.

As this example illustrates, being unable to initiate contact can keep you from taking advantage of unexpected opportunities, of meeting interesting new people, of developing new friendships, of hours of fascinating conversation, and of untold pleasure.

You have the right to risk reaching out to other people and attempt to initiate contact. That doesn't mean they will always respond in the way you want them to, but you never know until you try. Most people enjoy meeting and conversing with others. You will probably be greeted with warm smiles, gestures which indicate a willingness to talk, disclosure of personal information, and even questions directed back at you.

It pays to reach out. You will make new friends. You will take advantage of more opportunities. You will make every event more special if you are not afraid to reach out to the other people who are there with you.

After a jazz concert by the Count Basie Band, my husband Ed was waiting near the set to see if he could talk with one of the musicians. Standing next to him was a young lady, also waiting. He asked who she was waiting to see, and she explained that she was a friend of Danny House, a sax player with the Basie band. They chatted while they waited. Soon Danny came out and the lady introduced Ed to Danny House. The three of them talked for a few minutes, during which Ed explained that in addition to being a jazz devotee, he was also a band teacher for a junior high school with a big band jazz program. Danny expressed an interest in doing a music clinic for the students. Ed and Danny exchanged telephone numbers.

A few months later Ed and Danny met at a jazz educators' conference to work out the final details for the music clinic. When they had finished, Danny introduced Ed to Byron Stripling, the lead trumpet player for the Count Basie Band, and they got acquainted over lunch. Later that same evening Byron introduced Ed to jazz saxaphonist Branford Marsalis (a Grammy Award winner) and suggested that Branford also do a clinic with Ed's band. Branford said he would be glad to do a clinic for free whenever he was in the area.

When Danny came to the junior high school for the music clinic and even played with them in their evening concert, the kids were greatly impressed and had individual pictures taken with him.

Later that same year when Branford was in San Diego, he came to the band room for an afternoon rehearsal, played with the band, and took time to talk with the students before his evening concert. They were excited when they saw "their friend" Branford on *The Arsenio Hall Show* a few nights later and again during the Grammy Awards later that same year.

Ed had given his students two wonderful, incredible experiences, all because he had dared to initiate contact with a young lady after a concert.

What opportunities are you missing because you are afraid to risk reaching out?

INITIATING CONTACT IS SCARY

There are several reasons people pleasers are afraid to initiate contact, or even to respond to contacts from others.

1. They don't think anyone would want to talk with them. People pleasers don't have a strong sense of self-esteem; therefore, they don't see themselves as being the least bit interesting to others. So they don't initiate conversations.

Remember the woman at the well in the fourth chapter of John? When Jesus initiated contact with her and asked for a drink of water, she was genuinely surprised. She wanted to know why He, a Jew, would talk with her, a Samaritan. She couldn't believe that He would consider her worthy of conversation. In those days, Jews didn't have dealings with Samaritans. In today's world, people pleasers raise similar mental barriers to keep themselves from initiating contact. "A person like that wouldn't want to talk to a person like me," they rationalize. And they let the moment pass.

2. They don't want to impose. People pleasers see initiating contact as imposing on others. They don't consider that they might be providing a brief, and welcome, distraction for the other person. They don't even consider that the other person might be lonely or shy, might want some information, or might enjoy sharing knowledge of a subject. Basically, people pleasers think that if the other person wanted contact with them, the other person would initiate it.

3. They don't want to be rejected. The biblical story of Esther may be the one instance where there was a true risk of danger in making contact. In those days, the king had a law that no one was to enter his private court without being summoned. If anyone dared to enter unsummoned, it was up to the king to decide whether that person would live or die. If he held out his sceptre, it meant life; if he did not, it meant death. Esther was asked to approach the king, without being summoned, in order to tell him of the plot against her people, the Jews. For her, initiating the contact was risky. Fortunately, the king loved her and held out his sceptre.

For us, the risk is minimal. We will not be put to death if our contact is not welcome! It is true that there may be times when, for one reason or another, people may not welcome our contact, but these occasions are rare. It may take a few moments of conversation for you to determine that another person is simply not interested in talking. If the person turns away, refuses to smile, gives curt responses, and asks no questions of you, your best option is probably to find someone else to reach out to.

Remember, however, that a person's unwillingness to talk does not necessarily mean that you are being rejected on a personal basis. The other person may not be having a good day, may have just received bad news, may be angry with someone else, may be distrustful of redheads (or whatever color of hair you have), or just be shy. Unless you have done something offensive toward the other person, do not take the rebuff as a personal rejection. It is not your problem. It belongs to the other person!

4. They are afraid they can't perform brilliantly. Kevin is an intelligent, well-educated man who is skilled in the art of conversation. He can express his feelings with unusual awareness and clarity. He listens attentively and approaches situations creatively with a unique, and often unusual, perspective which makes him very interesting. But he can only do this with someone he knows well. With people he doesn't know, he gets so anxious about his ability to perform brilliantly that his attempts at conversation often become bizarre. He makes inappropriate comments. He tries too hard to be clever and sometimes ends up being sarcastic and rude. Even as he recognizes that he is behaving strangely and driving people away from him, he can't seem to relax and just be himself. He wants so desperately to please. But at least Kevin tries to converse with strangers.

Susie, on the other hand, doesn't even try. She just knows that she won't make a good showing, that she will say something stupid or be embarrassed or boring, so she won't initiate contact at all.

People pleasers may respond either way. Or they may just be afraid that they might get a conversation started and then fail to keep it going. Whenever there is silence in a conversation, people pleasers become uncomfortable and take it upon themselves to fill in the gaps, even while feeling unable to do so brilliantly. The prospect is enough to keep many people pleasers from initiating contact altogether.

PREPARE TO INITIATE CONTACT

In order to successfully initiate contact, you must first do some preparatory work. Some guidelines for initiating contact follow.

1. Have several topics on which you can converse comfortably and intelligently. I grew up in the jungles of Brazil with a tribe of Indians. My experiences were unusual, and I could enthusiastically tell fascinating stories which were sure to be of interest to almost anyone. For years, that was my basic topic of conversation with strangers. I became a master of turning any conversation to Brazil within a few sentences.

At a party I would ask the person next to me if she had lived here long. Predictably, after she had told me how long she had lived in the city, she would ask me how long I had lived there. I would respond by telling how long I had lived there, but that I had lived all over, including several interesting years in Brazil. That usually generated a question from the other person, and I was off and running with my prepared stories.

If I saw someone carrying a current novel, I would ask if he read a lot. Whatever the answer, I would usually be asked, shortly thereafter, if I read a lot myself. I could then say that I didn't have much time for reading since I was making up for the lost years of learning I had missed by growing up in the jungle and not going to school. That would generate a few questions, and I was in business.

And on and on. I became a master at turning any conversation to Brazil.

Pinpoint two or three topics that you are familiar and comfortable with, and learn to turn conversations to these subjects. If your topic is a hobby, you can probably start by asking other people what they do in their spare time. Sooner or later, if the other person is interested in maintaining the conversation, you will be asked what you do. That gives you the opportunity to discuss your hobby.

If you have visited a foreign country, ask people what their favorite trip has been. When you are asked the reciprocal question, you are free to launch into your travelogue.

2. Initiate contact from close proximity. Yelling across the room to a slight acquaintance or a stranger, or even attempting to initiate conversation with a person across a wide banquet table may not be the most successful endeavor. It is best if you can be near enough to talk in a quiet, personal tone, and to engage in direct eye contact when talking together. So approach the person you want to initiate contact with, looking him or her straight in the eye, and begin the conversation. At banquets, turn to your neighbor for better success because you can be heard more easily.

3. Establish a common interest. With strangers, start the conversation at some common ground. This may be the weather, the party you are attending, the book he or she is carrying which you have read, a mutual friend, the music you are listening to, or the food you are enjoying. While it is great to be able to be scintillating, what you say isn't as significant as just engaging the person in conversation. Once you get the conversation started, you can keep it rolling by asking questions. Try to phrase your questions so that they can't be answered with a simple yes or no answer.

Don't say, "Do you like the shrimp dish?" Instead, ask, "How does this shrimp dish compare with others you have had?" You might even ask about your companion's favorite seafood restaurant. This invites a story, or an opinion, and opens up the conversation.

4. Use appropriate self-disclosure. When you ask a question, be prepared to respond if the question is posed back to you. Don't be afraid to give your opinions, explain your attitudes, express your ideas, and tell your stories. Give personal information about yourself which will contribute to the conversation. Don't respond with short, one-word answers, even if the question can be answered that way. Expand upon your answers with self-disclosure. Let the other person get to know a little about you and who you are.

However, you won't want to be inappropriate about your self-disclosure. I will never forget an interview I once had in preparation for a television show. The interviewer spent more time telling me about his personal life than he did interviewing me for the show. Some of the things he told me were so personal that I would blush to write them in a personal diary, let alone share them with a stranger. In fact, his disclosures were so personal, and so inappropriate, that I doubted the truth of most of them. I wondered why this conversation was taking place and considered terminating the interview. There are just some things which are private enough not to be shared outside of a close, personal relationship or a counseling session. Keep your self-disclosures at a level which is appropriate to the development of the contact you have initiated.

    5. Don't be afraid of the silence. There are bound to be periods of silence in conversations, particularly when the two parties don't know each other. Don't be so afraid of silence that you blurt out something inappropriate. Instead, look around for another topic which might be a common interest and start a "new" conversation with the other person. After a period of silence you might say something like, "I was just thinking . . . ," and complete the sentence appropriately.

    While most of the examples and information presented in this chapter have had to do with initiating contact with strangers, there can also be a hesitation to initiate contact with people one already knows.

    Joy, for instance, won't call any of her friends to invite them to go skiing or hiking with her. Even though she knows several of them enjoy these sports, she has many of the fears discussed above. She doesn't want to impose. She doesn't want to be rejected. She believes that if other people wanted to be with her, they would call and invite her.

    There are many reasons people are reluctant to interact with others. Leonard really likes Jake, one of his co-workers, and enjoys talking with him during coffee break. He has not, however, invited him to his home group or church because that is a deeper level of sharing than the two of them are used to having.

    When the problem with initiating contact involves deepening an existing relationship, the preparation includes valuing yourself enough to consider that the other person might like to have a closer relationship with you. It also includes taking care to time the request appropriately and taking the risk to make the request.

PRACTICE INITIATING CONTACT

The best way to get comfortable with a new behavior is to practice it in a safe setting. Think of situations in which you are having difficulty initiating contact. Consider how you might appropriately initiate contact. Write out what you would say. Rehearse aloud these situations in front of a mirror or while driving alone. Better yet, ask a friend to role-play with you. When you feel more comfortable with the new skills, start using them in real-life situations.

If you can't think of situations from your own life, here are some to use for practice.

1. You are at a party, and across the room you see a person who looks interesting. Initiate contact. (You might say, "I'd like to get to know you. We seem to have a lot in common. Would you like to get together next week and play golf?")

2. You are at a conference and notice a group of people talking with someone whose business ideas you greatly admire. You have always wanted to meet this person, and now is your chance.

3. You are sitting next to an interesting-looking person on a bus. He is carrying a book by one of your favorite authors. Initiate a conversation. (You might say, "I read that book. I particularly liked the way the author presented his ideas. What do you like best about what you have read so far?")

4. You love your new job, and one of your co-workers has impressed you with his knowledge of the company maze. Ask him to become your mentor.

9

Give and Receive Compliments

Coral, a people pleaser I know, isn't comfortable receiving compliments. She gets flustered, embarrassed, and uncomfortable, and usually blurts out something inappropriate. She may respond with shy denial ("Oh, no! Not me!") or with rejection ("Not this old rag, I've had it for years! It's all out of shape and the style is all wrong."). Then Coral usually finds something to compliment in return, thinking that a compliment must be repaid immediately. As strange as it may seem, although Coral desperately wants approval from others, she is afraid to accept it. So she does not handle compliments gracefully.

Gary seldom compliments others. He recognizes and appreciates a job well-done. He notices a neat appearance. He is pleased when a subordinate turns in a completed project, but he doesn't express his positive regard easily. Gary wants approval, but he believes that if he goes around complimenting others they will see him as someone who is ingratiatingly annoying.

A COMPARISON OF APPROACHES

Where you placed on the pleasing continuum in the self-tests at the beginning of this book will give you a better idea of your usual approach to giving and receiving compliments.

The *Me Only* person actively seeks compliments ("How did I do?") and asks people to confirm self-compliments ("I handled that well, didn't I?"). This person rarely gives compliments unless doing so gives him or her a sense of power or superiority over the other person. Any compliments given tend to be sarcastic ("I can see why they chose you for this job; it takes a real witch!") or barbed ("Most people wouldn't think that color was right for you, but I like it!").

The *Me First* person receives compliments with egotism ("I'm a terrific cook! Anything I try comes out well!"). This person may compliment others, but only if it doesn't take away from his or her own aggrandizement or remove him or her from the limelight.

The *We* person acknowledges compliments with either a simple thank you or a thank you with a touch of appropriate self-appreciation ("Thank you. I like this outfit also. It's my favorite."). This person can honestly express appreciation by giving a direct compliment.

The *You First* person often rejects compliments with self-deprecation or denial and then is effusive in complimenting the other person. However, this person continues to work hard to earn the compliments which he or she doesn't accept.

The *You Only* person may refuse compliments by arguing with the other person that the compliment is undeserved and untruthful, in spite of the fact that the approval is desperately wanted. This person is always working hard for approval, whether or not he or she accepts it. This person may either continually give compliments to everyone he or she meets or may behave in exactly the opposite way. The *You Only* person may think that no one would want his or her opinions anyway, including compliments.

GIVING AND RECEIVING COMPLIMENTS

Giving compliments and expressing appreciation for a job well done is a skill which needs to be developed. If you feel warm about someone or something which has been done, you have a right (and sometimes a responsibility) to say so. There are several reasons to let others know how you feel.

1. People enjoy hearing sincere, positive things about themselves. It makes you feel good to hear that someone approves of how you think, what you wear, something you have done, or who you are. A word of affirmation is an encouragement to continue your efforts in that direction.

I am sure that Jesus was pleased to hear His Father's approval given publicly, "This is my beloved Son, in whom I am well pleased" (Matt. 3:17).

2. Affirmation deepens relationships. When Paul wrote his letters to the churches, he usually started off with positive affirmations or compliments, such as "I thank my God upon every remembrance of you" (Phil. 1:3) and, "I thank God and pray always for you ever since I heard of your faith and the love which you have for all of the saints" (Col. 1:3–4, paraphrased). He wanted the Christians to know that their efforts were not unnoticed or unappreciated. He wanted to let them know how dear they were to him and how much he loved them in the Lord.

When you compliment someone sincerely, you usually find that the relationship progresses a little further than before. We all like to be appreciated, and we feel warm toward those who express that appreciation.

3. People who are complimented don't feel taken for granted. When Philip asked Nathanael to come and meet Jesus, Nathaniel was a little skeptical, but he went anyway. When Jesus saw them coming, He looked at Nathaniel and said, in essence, "There's a man in whom there is no guile!" What a compliment! I am sure that Nathaniel did not feel he was just another follower to Jesus at that moment, for Jesus had taken time to single him out and to give him a sincere compliment.

If your co-workers have helped you out, don't take it for granted or forget to acknowledge their assistance. Compliment them. If your children bring home A's, don't take it for granted, even if they are smart and always bring home top grades. Compliment them.

4. Sincere compliments make criticism easier to take. While you won't want to use compliments to get people off guard in order to criticize them, it is true that including a sincere compliment when there is negative feedback to give is a good way to affirm the person while trying to change behavior.

Jesus sometimes did this. Before he criticized the Pharisees for their failure to follow the law when it came to judgment, mercy, and faith, He did compliment them on their faithfulness in tithing (Matt. 23:23).

MISCONCEPTIONS ABOUT GIVING COMPLIMENTS

People who deliberately do not compliment others may subscribe to misconceptions about giving positive feedback.

1. People will be embarrassed. My friend Gail gets painfully embarrassed when someone singles her out for a compliment. She blushes, becomes incoherent, and stammers out a self-deprecating response. Because she gets so embarrassed, she assumes that others do, too. Therefore, she doesn't compliment others because she doesn't want to embarrass anyone.

2. People will think I want something. Because Gail is uncomfortable receiving compliments, she usually tries to pay them back with either a return compliment, a gift, or a pleasing behavior. She has the idea that if she compliments someone, the other person will think she wants something. Not wanting people to feel obligated to her, she rarely compliments others.

On the other hand, if she does want something from a friend, Gail begins her request by giving several compliments. In one instance, she gushed, "You are such a good seamstress. I could never sew like you can. I admire you so much. Would you help me with this sewing project?"

Compliments must not be used as cushions for requests, nor do compliments require repayment.

3. People know how I feel; I don't have to tell them. People don't know how you feel. Besides, even if you show a friend or partner that you truly care, he or she probably would like to hear the words. Even if you never criticize, the implied compliment isn't as sweet as the spoken word.

Solomon gave us several verses in Proverbs which would encourage us to be open about complimenting others. He says that good words make us feel good, are sweet to the soul, and are as precious as silver and gold (Prov. 12:25, 15:23, 16:24, 25:11).

4. People who are paid to do a good job shouldn't have to be complimented if they do it well. Joshua hates to tip. He firmly believes that a waitress, a steward on a cruise ship, a bell hop, anyone in a service-oriented job, ought to perform well because of the salary paid. If good service is given, Joshua takes it as his due and does not show his appreciation either verbally or monetarily.

As you have probably noticed, it is hard to get good service today. If someone goes out of his or her way to make your dining or traveling experience a good one, a compliment is in order. (So is a tip!)

MISCONCEPTIONS ABOUT RECEIVING COMPLIMENTS

There are many varied reasons people have difficulty receiving compliments.

1. I don't deserve the compliment. Sometimes when I receive a compliment, I don't feel as if I deserve it. I may not have lived up to my own expectations of how I wanted to look or what I wanted to be or achieve.

Difficulty in receiving compliments may be tied to a lack of positive self-esteem. If you do not feel good about yourself or your abilities, you are likely to reject any positive feedback you receive. Or if your expectations of yourself are too high and you are always falling short of those expectations, you will tend to discount any compliments received because, in your own opinion, you aren't good enough. If you are comparing yourself with others, you will always be able to find someone better. (Of course, you will also be able to find people who are not as good as you, but you will probably overlook this fact.)

2. People don't mean the compliment. Another issue behind the inability to receive compliments graciously is a strong need for the approval of others. For the people pleaser, the need for approval is so deep that one compliment is never enough, and the truth of a compliment is usually in doubt. Therefore, when a compliment is given, there is a mental warning which goes off alerting you that this is just *one* comment and not unconditional approval; therefore, it may not be worth accepting.

3. People will think I'm conceited. When asked why she didn't accept compliments about her piano playing, Alicia, a highly talented pianist, admitted she believes people would think she is conceited if she agreed with their assessment of her skill.

Paul says that, while we aren't to think of ourselves as more than we are, we must have an honest appraisal of who we are and what gifts God has given us (Rom. 12:3–8). It is not conceit to acknowledge that you have achieved a certain level of skill, become a good person, or accomplished something special.

4. Now I have to live up to this level of behavior. A compliment is not an expectation of continued performance, although the expectation may also exist. A compliment is a simple acknowledgment of a one-time behavior or a moment of perception about someone.

5. Compliments must be repaid. This belief has already been discussed. Suffice it to say that a compliment need not be returned with a gift or pleasing behavior.

PREPARE TO GIVE AND RECEIVE COMPLIMENTS

When learning to give compliments, keep in mind the following:

- Be sincere.

- Be brief—don't go overboard or become too effusive.

- Compliment the behavior, not the person. ("That was a thoughtful thing to do," not "You are such a thoughtful person.")

- Don't expect repayment for the compliment.

- Don't use sarcasm.

- Don't give barbed compliments.

- Sometimes it is nice to compliment in front of others.

When learning to receive compliments, you will want to remember the following:

- Don't deny the compliment.

- Don't put yourself down.

- Don't try to repay the compliment.

- Don't reject the compliment.

Learning to give or receive compliments graciously will take some practice because current habits have been developed over a period of years. But it is worth the effort to become gracious about compliments and open with your own expressions of appreciation. Try it—you'll like it.

PRACTICE GIVING AND RECEIVING COMPLIMENTS

The best way to be comfortable with a new behavior is to practice it in a safe setting. Think of situations in which you are having difficulty giving and receiving compliments. Write out what you could say. Rehearse aloud these situations in front of a mirror or while driving alone. Better yet, ask a friend to role-play with you. When you feel more comfortable with the new skills, start using them in real-life situations.

If you can't think of situations from your own life, use some of these to practice.

Giving Compliments

1. You have gone to a friend's home for dinner. The roast and fixings were terrific. Express your appreciation for the meal.

2. A friend cancels some important plans to come over and help you make a home repair. Thank her for her sacrifice. (You might say, "I want you to know how much I appreciate your coming over. You're a genuine friend.")

3. A friend has lost thirty pounds and looks great. Express your admiration for her perseverance.

4. A co-worker handles an angry client particularly well. Compliment him for his expertise at such a difficult task.

Receiving Compliments

1. You have made a good presentation in front of the executive staff at your company. Later, one of those attending compliments you. Respond appropriately. (You might say, "Thank you. I felt it went well.")

2. You took care of a friend's children for the afternoon, and she calls later to tell you how much fun her children said they had with you. Respond

appropriately. (You might say, "Thank you. I enjoyed being with them, too. I'm glad I could help you out.")

3. You planned a successful surprise party for your spouse. Some of the guests compliment you. Respond appropriately.

4. Your research and report saved the company a lot of money. The president compliments you. Respond appropriately.

10

Show Love and Affection

When I was single I visited a famous author at his invitation. I had never met him, but admired his work for years and wanted to use some of his ideas in a book I was writing. By reading the jacket of his latest book, I discovered where he worked. I called Information, got the telephone number, and called him. We chatted for a few minutes and he suggested that if I were ever in his city, I should visit him so we could talk further.

He sounded so warm and friendly on the telephone that when I discovered that I was scheduled to be in his city within the next month, I called him again and arranged a time to get together. We spent a whole day and evening together, discussing our writing, hashing out ideas, sharing with each other who we were and what our dreams were. He gave me a tour of his elaborate home and showed me his play room, which included various musical instruments, video games, two televisions hooked to video recorders, a pinball machine, and shelves of books. He was so real, so warm, so interesting that I enjoyed the time very much. I was impressed that someone as famous and successful as he would make time for me.

I was surprised when he confessed that he was lonely and hated his solitude. He told me of the different ways he went about finding people to be with. He said when all of his efforts to find company failed, he would console himself with a favorite treat, tuna fish with onions! I was touched by his openness. While I certainly wasn't romantically interested in him, I liked him. A lot. It was great to find someone who was open and honest right away.

When I got home, I wrote him a letter thanking him for the wonderful experience and for being so real with me. I told him that I had enjoyed getting to know him as a person, not just as a famous author. I shared specifically what I had liked about him. Then I finished, playfully—but probably at least halfway seriously—". . . and if you ever want someone to share an evening of tuna and onions with you, give me a call."

He never called. Several months later I was in his city again, and I called to see if he was free for a cup of coffee. He was busy, he said. Oh, and thank you for the nice letter. His tone of voice seemed wary, closed, and definitely cool. Waves of embarrassment rolled over me. I couldn't get off of the telephone quickly enough. I felt I had done something terribly wrong! I decided I had been forward and pushy. I wanted to vanish from the face of the earth. I wished I could unsend the letter. How awful!

Suddenly I stopped my destructive self-talk. I asked myself just what had I done that was so terrible? I had been caught expressing appreciation for someone. That's all. It was not a crime. I was not guilty of anything wrong. It was okay to say "I like you" to another person, whether or not they responded in kind. A little of my embarrassment faded, but not all of it. Believe it or not, for years whenever I thought of that wonderful afternoon and evening, I would start to burn with guilt over that letter. Once again I would have to speak firmly with myself to get past the embarrassment.

What kind of world do we make for ourselves when telling someone we like them becomes a source of guilt?

A Comparison of Alternatives

Where you placed on the pleasing continuum in the self-tests at the beginning of this book will give you a better idea of your usual approach to showing love and affection.

The *Me Only* person is often so interested in being told he or she is loved and appreciated, that there is little time for expressing positive regard for others. However, if this person does want to share affection for someone, there is little hesitation in the expression. There may be, however, a hint of "and aren't you lucky that I feel this way?" in what is said. Often when affection is expressed it is with the expectation that something similar will be expressed in return.

The *Me First* person also expects to be loved and appreciated, and is comfortable telling others that they are loved and appreciated—whenever it is necessary to let them know (to keep a partner happy, to keep favors coming).

The *We* person expresses love and affection in appropriate terms and at appropriate times. This person is not afraid to be the first to express feelings, and allows the other person to respond freely or to simply acknowledge the feelings which have been expressed.

The *You First* person, who is dying for love and affection, expresses these feelings in many ways in order to get people to like or love in return. Feelings might be expressed verbally, through gift-giving or personal sacrifices, in writing, by being of service and subservient, or by doing favors. The main reason for these expressions is to receive reciprocal love and affection. At the same time, when a *You First* person experiences genuine love and affection for another, there may be a reluctance to express these feelings for fear of rejection.

The *You Only* person seeks love and affection in the same way as the *You First* person, but there is a sense of desperation in the approach and an annoying excessiveness of expressions. This person sends too many cards and letters, comes to visit too often, does too many favors, calls too often, compliments *ad nauseum*—which can be more annoying than the slobbers of an overly-friendly puppy. Again, the *You Only* person who genuinely falls in love or who has strong personal feelings of affection for a friend may be unable to express these honestly.

APPROPRIATE EXPRESSIONS OF LOVE AND AFFECTION

People pleasers often do loving and affectionate things even when they do not feel that way inside. What they often feel is a need to be loved and appreciated, so they behave in ways designed to engender the responses they need. They use ingratiating behaviors as substitutes for genuine relational skills or caring. They are trying to buy love and affection. Unfortunately, they do not succeed.

Genuine love and affection cannot be bought. These are emotional responses to who we are as persons, not necessarily to what we do or what we give. If doing and giving grow naturally from our deep feelings, these behaviors are appropriate. But if the behaviors precede the feelings, they are inappropriate. This is not to say that we are not to be kind to one another, or to do favors for people we don't know well. We just shouldn't try to buy approval with our behaviors.

If you spend all of your time doing for others, you will not have time left over to take care of your own business, yourself, and your personal goals. You won't have time to follow the will of God for your life because you are spending your time living for the will of other people. So reevaluate your motives the next time you find yourself being overly affectionate without sincere feelings for the other person.

The irony of the situation is that when people pleasers experience a genuine sense of caring, they are often incapable of openly and honestly sharing those feelings for fear that they will be rejected if their feelings are not returned.

It is true that not everyone you like will like you back to the same degree. But don't let that stop you from letting people know that you sincerely admire, respect, like, or love them. Unless you make a pest of yourself, you will not be thought less of.

REASONS WE TRY TO BUY LOVE AND AFFECTION

People pleasers who express love and affection in order to win love and affection probably subscribe to the following beliefs:

1. *"People wouldn't like me if I didn't do these things."* For years Nathan gave everyone in the office little Christmas gifts. He started early in the year buying trinkets and mugs, and even making things for his co-workers. A couple of days before Christmas he would go around the office giving each person a gift and expressing his affection for them. Each year Nathan received a little gift back from most of the people in the office. Nathan loved Christmas. He felt so loved and appreciated.

One year Nathan had unusually high personal expenses. Money was tight. He couldn't afford even the small gifts he had given in the past. That year, he handmade his Christmas cards for each person in the office, but there were no gifts to be given. He went around as before, giving out the cards and telling people how much he loved and appreciated them. He received very few gifts that year. It was a terrible Christmas. Nathan vowed then and there that even if he had to give up lunches for months, he would never again give up his gift giving. He wasn't going to miss out on feeling loved and appreciated.

Nathan was trying to buy affection. Yet what he failed to see was that most of the gifts he had received in the past were motivated by guilt. Some people, when they receive a gift, give one back so they won't feel guilty. Nathan was not getting genuine love and affection from most of the people at the office.

Because favors and gifts and "I like yous" tend to be returned in kind, people pleasers do *appear* to be successful in their quest for love and affection. But upon closer inspection, what they are receiving is often merely a polite response rather than deep emotional relationships. Therefore, when people pleasers stop these behaviors, they do experience a loss of some of the reciprocal behaviors. This may be interpreted as a loss of love and affection. It is not. You can't lose what you never had!

2. *"I am not worthy of being loved for just being me."* Liz will do anything for anyone. If someone needs a yard mowed, an errand run, a package wrapped, a child watched, or a repair completed, Liz is the person to call. But Liz isn't comfortable just *being* with someone. So Liz isn't good at visiting sick friends, "hanging out" together, walking along the beach, or sitting on a park bench with friends. Liz doesn't feel worthy of being liked or loved for just being. Liz has to *do*.

3. *"I like doing nice things for people. This is who I am."* Sally won't admit that she does loving things in order to earn love and affection. She thinks she does these things simply because she likes to. But Sally sometimes gets depressed when she thinks that no one genuinely loves and appreciates her.

There are times when we do things for people just because we like doing them, and we aren't expecting any major return on our investment. That's good. We need to be kind one to another (Eph. 4:31–32). The problem arises when we do kind things when we don't want to; then we begin to resent the lack of returned feelings.

REASONS WE WON'T EXPRESS GENUINE LOVE AND AFFECTION

There are several excuses people pleasers use to justify why they aren't comfortable expressing genuine love and affection.

1. *My feelings might be misunderstood.* One reason I was embarrassed about my letter to the author was that I interpreted the coolness in his voice when I called him later to mean that he had misunderstood my intentions in the letter. I wasn't interested in

dating him, or becoming romantically involved. I only wanted to perhaps become his friend.

One lady I know was seriously misunderstood. She had grown up in a family where love and affection were never expressed, and so she had learned to suppress her feelings. At the age of thirty, she went to a seminar where the participants were challenged to express genuine love and affection. That night, she got in touch with deep feelings of love for her family and sat up until after midnight writing each brother and sister a personal letter. She told each one what she appreciated about him or her. She ended each letter with, "I love you very much and I always will." The next morning she mailed the letters and went to work humming a happy little tune.

Later in the week the telephone wires buzzed as her brothers and sisters called each other from all over the United States. They compared letters and impressions, and finally everyone agreed. There was only one possible explanation for receiving such letters. And only one thing to do. They called the police in the town where the lady lived, gave her name and address, and asked that an officer be sent over to check on her. Such strange behavior could only be interpreted as a last desperate attempt to reach out and touch someone before she committed suicide!

It was hard to tell who was the more surprised, the lady or the police when they showed up at her door and found her happy and well!

Fortunately, such misunderstandings are rare.

2. *"I might be rejected."* Yes, that is true. But it is also a possibility that you won't be!

Daphne had a tremendous crush on a guy at college. She found every excuse to bump into him, to be with him, and to sit next to him. He was friendly, but unresponsive to her obvious attraction to him.

Daphne wrote him a letter expressing her feelings for him. He returned her letter with a kind but firm statement that he appreciated her regard, but that he didn't feel attracted to her and did not want a romantic relationship with her.

Daphne continued writing him letters until one day she wrote that if she couldn't have him, she didn't think she could go on living. It took counseling for Daphne to get over her depression.

It is unrealistic to expect that everyone we like will feel the same way toward us. So, if we are expressing love and affection only to be loved in return, we are sometimes going to experience rejection. But if we take small steps in the beginning and test the relationship as it grows, we can pick up on the early signs that our positive regard is not returned and can back off before someone feels it necessary to reject us outright.

3. *"It's just not done, saying what I feel."* For a long time in our culture it has not been acceptable for men to express their emotions—sometimes even including genuine love and affection. It just isn't done. Oh, it is okay for a man to pursue and court a woman with love and affection, but not to let another male friend know how strongly he feels toward him. I am glad to see that we are changing as a society and are more accepting of "male bonding" and expressions of emotion between men.

Some women also find it difficult to express their friendships in words. But there is nothing wrong with an open display of love and affection.

Remember how the woman came into the dinner at Simon's house and cried over Jesus' feet, dried them with her hair, then anointed Jesus' feet with expensive ointment (Luke 7:36–50)? Her expression of affection was unusual, but not rejected.

Jesus did not consider it unmanly to express love and affection. At the Last Supper, He was affectionate with John, one of His special friends (John 13:23;

21:20, 24). And John wrote to us that we ought to love one another, for love is of God (1 John 4:7–8).

Expressing feelings and emotions is appropriate. Do it!

4. "I am afraid." You may have vague fears about what will happen if you express genuine love and affection. You may be afraid that you will embarrass someone, that you will be considered pushy, that you ought not to make the first move, that you will become too vulnerable, or that your expressions will not be appreciated.

Identify your fears and ask yourself what is the worst that could happen if those things did occur. Next ask yourself if those fears are realistic. If they are, consider how you can phrase your expressions of love and affection so that none of those things will occur. With proper planning you will considerably reduce your risks.

PREPARE TO SHOW LOVE AND AFFECTION

If you have decided to stop being loving and affectionate only as a means of obtaining love and affection and have decided to risk expressing genuine feelings of love and affection, you will want to follow the following guidelines:

1. Be clear about how you feel. Ask yourself what it is about the other person that you admire, respect, like, or love. Analyze your feelings and be sure that what you feel is genuine. Has the other person achieved something you'd like to achieve? Is the other person someone you want to be like? Are there things about that person that make you feel warm, appreciated, included, excited, enthusiastic, and motivated? Do you enjoy being with the other person because of his or her listening skills, patience, calmness, strength, or sense of humor? Think through what it is you want to acknowledge about that other person.

2. Don't gush. Having always wanted to be a writer, I grew up with an awe for writers. When I first started writing, I was assigned to work with an author-turned-editor whose writing I had admired. When I was introduced, I grabbed his hand, and blurted, "I am *so* glad to meet you! I think you're terrific! I loved your book! This is so exciting I can hardly stand it!"

He couldn't have looked more shocked if I had dumped a bucket of cold water over his head! But he smiled, and after a few moments the awkwardness passed. My words were sincere. But they were a bit much! It would have been better to express my admiration and respect with a little less exuberance until I got to know the editor better.

Say what you feel, but don't gush.

3. Don't have unreasonable expectations. Mabel had a problem. She had met a nice lady named Janet who had instantly decided that Mabel was her new best friend. Janet attached herself to Mabel and became jealous of any time Mabel spent with anyone else. Mabel didn't return Janet's feelings. She already had several close friends as well as a "best friend" of long standing. Janet had unrealistic expectations.

If you like someone, let that person know. But don't be surprised if that person doesn't necessarily like you as much as you like him or her. Be willing to express how you feel without exerting pressure on the other person. Let the friendship grow naturally, and you may find that your feelings are reciprocated. Then again, you may not.

Also, just because you are open about how you feel doesn't mean that other people are going to be as open about how they feel. They may enjoy hearing how much you care about them, but then not give you a clue about how much they like you! Learn to accept people where they are in their own journey toward being open about their positive feelings, and don't expect them to be where you would like them to be.

Putting an end to your behavior of trying to earn love and affection is a scary thing because some of the responses you have been receiving may stop. Learning to express genuine love and affection is scary, as well, because people may not respond in the way you hope they will. But taking these steps will bring you closer to being more in charge of your own life as you take responsibility for who you are and what you feel.

PRACTICE SHOWING LOVE AND AFFECTION

The best way to get comfortable with a new behavior is to practice it in a safe setting. Think of situations in which you are having difficulty showing love and affection to someone. Consider how you might appropriately show love and affection. Write out what you would say. Rehearse aloud these situations in front of a mirror or while driving alone. Better yet, ask a friend to role-play with you. When you feel more comfortable with the new skills, start using them in real-life situations.

If you can't think of situations from your own life, here are some to use for practice.

1. A co-worker has just lost her spouse. Express a genuine level of caring.

2. An artist you respect greatly is performing at your church. You have an opportunity to meet him. Express your sincere appreciation for his work.

3. You have an acquaintance with whom you would like to become better friends. Tell that person how you feel. (You might say, "You seem like a very

special and interesting person, and I'd like to get to know you better. Would you be free to come over for dinner one night next week?")

4. Your parents are visiting from out of town. Tell them how much they mean to you.

Part IV

*Love Life—
Become
Whole*

11

Set and Achieve Life-Changing Goals

Bonnie, Glenn, and Rita came to one of my seminars on people-pleasing behaviors. Bonnie left with several pages of notes. She had been very impressed with what had been presented, and had determined to make changes in her lifestyle. No longer would she be a self-destructive people pleaser. During the next couple of weeks, Bonnie reviewed the notes and often caught herself in time to make a positive choice instead of instinctively falling into her old habit of people-pleasing behaviors. But it wasn't long until Bonnie's initial enthusiasm faded, and she stopped reading the notes. Soon she was back into her habitual people-pleasing patterns.

Glenn also left with several pages of notes, which he threw into the front seat of his car along with his jacket, a couple of books he bought, and a package of potato chips. He had identified with a lot of what was shared in the seminar, and he mulled over some of the ideas as he drove home. He stuffed the notes into an already-full desk drawer, promising himself that one day he would take a closer look at them. But he never did.

Rita's approach was different. Rita's notes went home with her, but they were placed in the center of her desk. During the next two weeks, Rita carefully evaluated her lifestyle, selected several areas in which she wanted to make changes, wrote specific goals for how and when she would make these changes, and developed a step-by-step life-changing plan. Rita implemented the plan one step at a time. Now, one year later, Rita is a different person. She is more self-confident, motivated, pleasant, and independent. She has sought out new areas of ministry and has been successful. She has made new and healthy relationships. Rita walks taller, smiles more sincerely, and is fun to know.

Because she set specific goals and followed through on her plans, Rita changed her life. Because they did not set appropriate goals, Bonnie and Glenn did not experience the changes they said they wanted.

WHY SET GOALS?

Pretend that it is suddenly one year from now. Your life is exactly the same as it is today. Nothing has changed. You haven't grown. You haven't tried to reach out to anyone new. You haven't started a new ministry. You haven't read any new books, lost weight, made new friends, or completed that degree. You have not begun to control your anger, depression, fears, or insecurities. You are still living your life for other people instead of doing what you want to do—or even what God would have you do. How do you feel? Happy? Suicidal?

If you do not develop a plan and do something different, your life will be pretty much the same in the future as it is today. Of course, you can choose to continue in the same patterns you have been living. Or you can choose, as Rita did, to make life changes in areas which you feel need to be improved. The first three chapters of this book outline the problems with being a people pleaser, whose main goal in life is to please others. Chapters 4–10 give specific ways to break free from self-destructive people-pleasing habits. Although the choice is yours to make, I would recommend that you take a look at any of those areas in which you would like to make your life better and choose to make changes. Don't be like the person who looks in the mirror, sees a smudge on his face, and then walks away without doing anything, forgetting what he saw (read James 1:22–25). Choose to wipe away the smudge. Become the beautiful person God designed you to be.

Goals are a necessary part of our lives.

1. Goals provide a direction for our energies. Now that Rita has a set of goals, she knows where to center her personal-growth energy. She isn't using a shotgun approach to "fix" her life. Her actions are carefully directed and follow a logical pattern toward achieving her stated goals.

Remember the story of Naomi and Ruth? Naomi had a goal. She wanted Ruth to marry a nice Jewish man. So she went about advising Ruth and encouraging her until Ruth agreed. Naomi got Ruth to help her achieve a goal she had set for Ruth (Ruth 2–4).

Paul told Timothy he ought to have a goal of becoming unashamed before God and approved of by God, rightly discerning the truth of the Word of God (2 Tim. 2:15). What does God's Word have to say to you

about how you have been living your life ? Do you need
to set goals to make any changes?

2. *Goals help us make choices.* My husband Ed
tells about how this works. Years ago, Motel 6 would take
reservations but would not guarantee them past 6:00 P.M.,
and would not use a credit card to hold them. You either
showed up with cash by 6:00 P.M. or you lost your room.
So if your goal was to stay at the Motel 6 during a trip
across the county, you made decisions during the day
which would ensure that you were at the motel by 6:00
P.M.. Early in the day you might take attractive side trips
and detours. But as the time grew nearer, no side trip,
no matter how tempting, would be even considered if it
would keep you from reaching your goal on time.

Our goals will help us make correct choices
in other areas of our lives. When presented with two
choices, the one which is going to help us achieve our
goals will be the one we are most likely to choose *if we
are genuinely committed to reaching our goals*, and if
we keep them clearly before us.

Nehemiah had a choice. He could have stayed
in the king's house, comfortable and cared for. But he
had a goal. He wanted to return to Jerusalem and rebuild the city. He chose to take on a difficult task, an
unpopular task which would be opposed by the sur-
rounding tribesmen, a task which required a lot of hard
work. But Nehemiah knew what he wanted and made
a choice (Neh. 2:1–6:19).

3. *Goals need to be realistic.* Bonnie honestly
thought that when she left the seminar she was going
to be different overnight. And she was, for a few days.
But it is not realistic for her to expect that she would
be able to make a number of permanent life changes
just by making one decision to do so. Rita was more
realistic because she knew that life changes involve a
series of small steps, a lot of work, and time before they
become natural and comfortable.

4. Goals give us a feeling of sucess when we achieve them. Solomon tells us that hard work will bring us a sense of accomplishment, and that when our heart's desires are accomplished it is sweet to our souls. (Prov. 13:11, 19). There is little as satisfying as having a list and checking off things as they are accomplished. The more steps we can mark off as accomplished on our goal lists, the more self-confident we become, the more committed we become to the process, and the more we see the rewards in our lives.

5. Goals can provide energy. One of the most amazing aspects of goal-setting is that when we are truly committed to achieving a particular goal, we actually have the physical and psychological energy we need to reach that goal. And when we finally reach the goal, the extra energy seems to evaporate. The energy is created when we have a firm picture of what we want to be real in our lives.

Surely you have had experience with this. Have you ever come home so tired that it even hurt to breathe? All you wanted to do was somehow get home to the recliner, slip off your shoes, and collapse. You didn't want to eat. You didn't want to talk. You just wanted to sit and be left alone until it was time to crawl into bed. You even considered sleeping in the chair if getting to the bed was too much trouble. So what if the kids had left cereal spilled on the kitchen floor and milk spoiling on the table? So what if the place looked as if a hurricane had blown through it? You just didn't care.

Then the telephone rang and on the other end were friends you hadn't seen in years. They were in town for the evening and would like to come over for a while. They could be at your house in twenty minutes!

Suddenly, as you looked around the room, you realized that it was not your goal to have your friends see your house looking as it did. You goal was to have a clean and pleasant environment in which to receive your friends. Gone was your lethargy. Gone was your inability to move. Suddenly, your adrenalin shot up and you began to move with the speed of lightning. The dishes were gathered into the dishwasher. The kids' clothes were scooped up and hid in the washing machine. The milk was tossed and the cereal cleaned up, the vacuum skimmed over the carpet, and a dust rag cleared off the accumulated dust. The bathroom got the once over, and the newspapers were tossed in the garage. Within nineteen minutes, you had accomplished the impossible and were ready to great your guests with a smile and a fresh pot of coffee.

How did you do that? You had a goal that the current reality did not match. Until it did, you had sufficient energy to effect the change.

When you go on a diet, you will have sufficient psychological energy to resist problem foods as long as you are committed to your goal of losing weight. When you achieve your goal, unless you set another goal to maintain that weight, your psychological energy will vanish and you will no longer resist the problem foods. And you may just have to diet again.

I remember when I set a goal to get a graduate degree. I was a single parent raising two sons. I had a full-time job. I had to work overtime to pay for my tuition, and I taught a community college class one night a week. During those two years I also wrote five books and edited a magazine for single adults. Just thinking about that time in my life makes me tired today. It was exhausting, but I had the physical, mental, and psychological energy required to reach my goal. As soon as I reached the goal, I was too tired to take on any other responsibilities, even though there were significantly less demands upon my time.

I am reminded of Samson, whose last goal in life was to destroy the Philistines. He prayed that God would grant his last wish, and he was given sufficient energy (power, strength) to accomplish his goal. He pulled down the house, killing over three thousand enemies of Israel as well as himself (Judg. 16:23–31). We also have access to the power of God to give us the strength to accomplish our goals, particularly if they are in line with what God would have us accomplish.

6. *Goals give us a way to check what we are becoming.* Without goals, what you are to become is a hit-and-miss proposition. With goals, your progress is planned, and your progress can be measured. We all like to be measured. Kids are always asking that we measure how tall they are so they can see how much they have grown. Those self-assessment quizzes in popular magazines are there because most of us cannot resist measuring ourselves. I even took one once which asked, "What kind of a husband are you?" I just couldn't resist seeing how I came out on the scoring! We all like to measure our progress.

When setting goals, you will want to be sure that you are genuinely committed to them, and then count the cost to your time and energies and other areas of your life (Luke 14:28–30). Make sure the goals are realistic so you can be successful in reaching them.

WHY WE DON'T SET GOALS

There are several reasons people don't set goals in their lives.

1. *They are too busy.* Everyone is busy these days. Our lives are awfully full. Some people are busy rushing around pleasing others. Others are busy loafing. Still others are busy with mundane chores. But is your life full of what you want it to be? Yes, setting goals is hard work, and it does take a lot of time, thought, and energy. But the payoff is terrific. Don't be too busy to set goals.

2. They are too lazy. Glenn, the man who attended my seminar and threw his notes in the seat of his car, plans to set goals—someday, but not today. He thinks that one day he will have some extra energy and will awaken all fired up to make life changes. Until then, he will just relax, rest, and continue to put it off.

3. They are afraid of commitment and accountability. Judy needs to lose thirty pounds. But she won't actually go on a diet because she isn't ready to make that much of a commitment to a goal. Also, the last time Judy went on a diet she announced it to her co-workers—and then every time she ate something fattening, someone reminded her that she was supposed to be on a diet. Judy hated that. So now Judy doesn't set goals because she doesn't want to make a commitment she can't live up to.

4. They are afraid of failure. Another reason Judy doesn't set a goal to lose her thirty pounds is that she isn't sure she can do it. She is afraid of failure. Rather than risk the failure, Judy would rather not start a diet at all.

The goal-setting process can result in failure if:

- the commitment isn't strong enough (The desired mental picture isn't clear enough to make the current reality unacceptable.)

- the goals are unrealistic (Judy wants to lose the thirty pounds in one month.)

- there is low or no self-esteem, and the person doesn't feel worthy of achieving the goal in the first place.

But people don't have to fail when setting goals. They just need to recognize on what their fears are based, eliminate the problems, and then set appropriate goals.

SET APPROPRIATE GOALS

What does an appropriate goal look like? There are four characteristics of an appropriate goal.

1. It is realistic. A realistic goal is one which is under your control and can be accomplished by you. Part of the realism is setting reasonable time frames for achieving the goal. Be sure the goals you are setting are realistic for you in that they are also the goals God would have you work on.

David had an unrealistic goal. He wanted to build a temple for the Lord. But God said He didn't want David to build it because David had been a man of war and God wanted a man of peace to build the temple. That would be Solomon. So David set a more realistic goal, that of amassing the supplies needed to build the temple. In that goal he was very successful (1 Chron. 22:1–10).

It is not realistic to become a different person overnight, but it is realistic to plan a series of small steps over a long period of time so that you will be a different person next year. A realistic goal is one that is attainable.

Part of the reason a goal is attainable is that you break it down into small, achievable steps. Learning a foreign language may be your goal, but the steps might include taking a class each semester, learning three hundred vocabulary words each semester, writing two pages a week in the new language, finding someone to speak the new language with, reading one newspaper article in the new language each week, and finally, reading a book in the new language. These small steps will help you reach the goal of becoming fluent in a new language.

2. It is measurable. Some goals are easier to measure than others, but if you don't have a way of measuring your progress, your goal is inappropriate.

"Becoming less of a people pleaser" is not an appropriate goal, for how will you know when you have succeeded?

Measurable means how much, how long, how high, how many, or how often. "I will say no five times this week when presented with unreasonable requests" is a measurable goal.

3. It is dated. Unless goals are dated, they have little value, for there is no urgency on reaching them. For a project, the date to be given is an *ending* date: "I will have read two books on self-esteem by the end of the month." For a process, the date to be given is a *beginning* date: "I will read my Bible for thirty minutes a day for the rest of my life, beginning today." (If you miss a day, you simply reaffirm the goal and continue the process. In order to celebrate process goals, you will want to set time periods such as one week or one month to check your progress. If you have successfully stayed with the process, then celebrate. Keep evaluating and celebrating periodically.)

Make sure your dates are realistic. Don't set yourself up for failure. Also make sure that they are urgent enough to keep the challenge before you. Don't set a year-long goal for something it ought to take only a couple of weeks to accomplish.

4. It is written. Mental goals are easily forgotten, ignored, and delayed. Write down your goals and keep copies where you can review them frequently. One copy goes into your Bible. One in your wallet or purse. One in your desk, and one where you can see it daily.

WHAT TO DO WITH YOUR WRITTEN GOALS

Just setting appropriate goals is not enough to effect life changes. There are several steps to take once you have written your goals.

1. *Pray over your goals daily.* Each day, as you have your daily devotions or quiet time with God, take out your goals and pray that you will have the wisdom, strength, and commitment to achieve your goals. Ask for guidance. Ask for the power of the Holy Spirit in your life. Paul says we are to not be anxious, but in every thing come to God with prayer and supplication, making our requests known to God (Phil. 4:6).

2. *Get a strong mental picture of what it will be like when you achieve your goal.* Sit in a quiet place and picture what it will be like when you have accomplished what you want to do. Remember a time in your past when you accomplished something you wanted very much. Experience the good feelings you had about yourself and then apply those same good feelings to your mental image of what it will be like when you achieve your goals. Feel how good it will be. Enjoy the picture.

What you want to do is to make the goal so attractive and so strong that you will have sufficient energy to reject the current reality and to keep striving toward the goal.

I was in the process of writing a book about fear when I realized I needed to do something I was frightened of in order for me to prove that what I was saying in the book was true. So I decided to go sky diving. The very thought of that petrified me. Every time I thought about the idea, I would break out in a cold sweat. But I had an appointment made for me to make the jump. At first, when I thought of jumping, I saw myself at the open door of the plane and scared to death. Then I realized that I wasn't following the proper principles. I asked myself if I had ever done anything like that before. "No!" I told myself. But that wasn't true. I did remember jumping on a trampoline in high school, and turning a forward flip. It was scary, but I did it and it felt exciting. I began picturing myself at the door of the plane, leaning forward and doing a forward flip,

coming up in the free-fall position, and feeling the ex-
hilaration of the forward flip on the trampoline. I went
through the experience forty or fifty times a day, picturing myself making the flip, and feeling the
excitement. After each mental "jump" I would say to
myself, "This is fun!" By the time I was actually kneel-
ing at the open door of the plane, the mental picture
was strong enough to keep me from being afraid. This
was not my first jump, it was more like my four thou-
sandth jump because I had created such a strong mental
picture. (The jump was a success, I am pleased to say.)

What will you be like when you have made
the life changes you want to make? What will it feel
like? How excited will you be? Picture it. Paint in the
emotion. Experience it daily, and your goals will be
strong enough to get you through any temptation to
abandon them.

*3. Eliminate all possible activities which are
not goal related.* All of us have to do things which are
not necessarily related to our current goals. We cook,
clean, wash clothes, take care of the children, work,
work out, spend time with friends, and do many other
things. Most of these do relate to goals: we want to be
clean, responsible, financially secure, physically fit, and
so on. But some activities may not contribute to any
significant goal: watching television, reading fiction, sun
bathing, chatting on the telephone for hours each night,
sleeping more than eight hours a night, taking naps.
Many of these types of activities can be eliminated and
replaced with goal-directed activities. Sometimes we
may even choose to temporarily "uncommit" ourselves
to prior goals in order to have more time to devote to
achieving new goals. For a specified time period we
might give up singing in the choir, serving on the PTA,
or participating in a community theater.

4. Follow the plan. While you may find it
necessary to revise your plan, if there is a change of

circumstance you won't want to revise it casually. For example, if you have set a goal to take a certain college class this semester, but the college doesn't offer it., you may have to revise your plan and spend this semester reading books and take the class next semester. But don't revise the plan just because you don't feel like taking the next step.

When you are tempted to abandon a goal, instead of giving in to that temptation, spend time reworking your mental picture of how great it will be when you achieve the goal. Spend time in prayer over the goal, and ask for renewed commitment.

5. *Celebrate your successes.* Because making life changes will involve many small steps, you will want to set milestones along the way to celebrate your successes when you have made significant achievements. These celebrations will encourage you to continue in your plan.

THE CHOICE IS YOURS

What are you going to become during this next year? What people-pleasing behaviors will you abandon? What behaviors will you develop to replace them? What will you learn? What new friends will you make? What relationships will change? What goals will you reach? The choice is yours.

You can do virtually anything you set your mind to do if the accomplishment is within your control, if you break it into small enough steps and commit yourself to the goal.

How will you be different one year from today? Remember:

"The difference between who you are and who you become is what you do." —*Harold Ivan Smith*

"What you are to be, you are becoming."

—*Anonymous*

Rom. 8:29 says that God wants us to be conformed to the image of His Son. How are you doing?

GOAL-SETTING WORKSHEET

Consider your lifestyle. In what areas do you want to become better? Take each of the seven areas addressed in this book and describe yourself. If you are satisfied with where you are, great! If you aren't, then set an overall goal to change that area of your life. Under each goal, write a couple of small steps which will assist you in achieving the goal you have written.

1. Expressing Your Opinions

A. "Do I express my opinions?" Describe when you do, and when you don't. List people with whom you are comfortable expressing your opinions, and people with whom you are uncomfortable.

_____

_____

_____

_____

_____

B. Write a goal about expressing your opinions.

_____

_____

_____

_____

C. Write three or four small steps which will lead you to the above goal.

_____

_____

_____

_____

_____

2. Confronting Productively

A. "Do I confront productively?" Describe when you do, and when you don't. List people with whom you are comfortable confronting, and people with whom you are uncomfortable.

_____

_____

_____

_____

_____

B. Write a goal about confronting productively.

_____

_____

_____

_____

_____

C. Write three or four small steps which will lead you to the above goal.

_____

_____

_____

_____

_____

3. Asking for What You Want

A. "Do I ask for what I want?" Describe when you do, and when you don't. List people with whom you are comfortable asking for what you want, and people with whom you are uncomfortable.

_____

_____

_____

_____

_____

B. Write a goal about asking for what you want.

_____

_____

_____

_____

_____

C. Write three or four small steps which will lead you to the above goal.

_____

_____

_____

_____

_____

4. Refusing Unreasonable Requests

A. "Do I refuse unreasonable requests?" Describe when you do, and when you don't. List people with whom you are comfortable refusing unreasonable requests, and people with whom you are uncomfortable.

_____

_____

_____

_____

_____

B. Write a goal about refusing unreasonable requests.

_____

_____

_____

_____

_____

C. Write three or four small steps which will lead you to the above goal.

_____

_____

_____

_____

_____

5. Initiating Contact

A. "Do I initiate contact?" Describe when you do, and
when you don't. List people with whom you are
comfortable initiating contact, and people with
whom you are uncomfortable.

_____

_____

_____

_____

_____

B. Write a goal about initiating contact.

_____

_____

_____

_____

_____

C. Write three or four small steps which will lead
you to the above goal.

_____

_____

_____

_____

6. Giving and Receiving Compliments

A. "Do I give compliments to others?" Describe when you do, and when you don't. List people to whom you are comfortable giving compliments and people with whom you are uncomfortable.

_____

_____

_____

_____

_____

B. Write a goal about giving compliments.

_____

_____

_____

_____

C. Write three or four small steps which will lead you to the above goal.

_____

_____

_____

_____

_____

D. "Do I receive compliments graciously?" Describe when you do, and when you don't. List people from whom you are comfortable receiving compliments and people with whom you are uncomfortable.

_____

_____

_____

_____

_____

E. Write a goal about receiving compliments.

_____

_____

_____

_____

F. Write three or four small steps which will lead you to the above goal.

_____

_____

_____

_____

7. Showing Love and Affection

A. "Do I show genuine love and affection?" Describe when you do, and when you don't. List people with whom you are comfortable showing genuine love and affection, and people with whom you are uncomfortable.

_____

_____

_____

_____

_____

B. Write a goal about showing genuine love and affection.

_____

_____

_____

_____

_____

C. Write three or four small steps which will lead you to the above goal.

_____

_____

_____

_____

_____

D. "Do I show love and affection I don't feel in order to buy approval?" Describe when you do, and when you don't. List people with whom you find yourself pretending love and affection in order to buy their approval.

_____

_____

_____

_____

_____

E. Write a goal about stopping pretending love and
affection in order to buy approval.

_____

_____

_____

_____

F. Write three or four small steps which will lead
you to the above goal.

_____

_____

_____

_____

_____

12

Live Free

"I want my life back!" Paula exclaimed to me one afternoon. "I am tired of having given away my power and control of my life. My happiness can't continue to depend upon whether or not other people approve of me! I can't always look around for someone to give me the 'go ahead' nod before I make a decision. I want to be free to live my own life!"

THE CHOICE IS YOURS

Perhaps you can identify with Paula. Perhaps you, too, are ready to eliminate the people-pleasing behaviors from your own life. Perhaps you want to discover power, excitement, and inspiration from within. Perhaps you want to become a whole person, not a half person always having to lean on someone else, always needing to be bolstered up by the approval of others. The choice is yours. You have to decide, *I want to do this!* No one can decide for you.

But if you do decide to make a change, some steps can help.

1. Affirm your self-esteem. You are a wonderfully created being, personally designed by God (Ps. 139:13–16). You are unique. Therefore, no one else knows how you should be. Only God knows just how much you can grow, how far you can go, and how much you have to contribute. Seek His input and His approval. You are a child of God, His heir, and a joint-heir with Jesus Christ (Rom. 8:14–17). Yours is a legacy of a power, not a spirit of fear! You are part of the body of Christ, an equal member with every other member (1 Cor. 12:12–27). You have a responsibility to become all you can be through the power of the Holy Spirit working in you and through you. Remember how the power of the Holy Spirit changed the disciples from simple workers to powerful preachers (Acts 1:8, 2:1–14)?

Ask God to search your heart and to bring to your mind any nonproductive self-talk so you can turn it into positive affirmations. If you have been telling yourself people won't like you unless you work hard to please them, begin telling yourself that people will like who you are becoming as you work to become conformed to the image of the Lord Jesus Christ. If you have been telling yourself you aren't worthy of being loved, remind yourself that God loved you so much that He gave His own Son to redeem you. You are worthy!

Some beliefs go so deep that just giving yourself a positive affirmation will not eradicate the old belief. Instead, you will have to challenge the truth of the old belief. Ask yourself:

"Is this true?"

"Who said so?"

"Did that person have all of the facts?"

"Have the facts changed since then?"

"Can I change the facts or reality now so the belief is no longer valid?"

Keep asking similar questions until you can find a chink in the armor protecting the old belief. When you find the chink, attack the weakness and break the power the old belief has over you. Remember that the old beliefs developed over a period of years, and making substitutions may also take a long time.

Search your heart. Are there problem attitudes or perspectives which you need to rethink? Have you been indifferent? Decide to be purposeful in your life. Have you been indecisive? Choose to make decisions. Eliminate worry, self-doubt, overcaution, pessimism, and complaining from your approach to life. You will have to start valuing yourself before you can expect others to recognize and respond to your value as a person.

Paul said that every aspect of our lives can be important. It is not just the spiritual side of us that is critical. We are encouraged to do everything we do heartily, as unto God, even when we eat and drink (Col. 3:17, 23; 1 Cor. 6:19–20, 10:31).

2. Become motivated. Eileen can point to a specific day when she decided to make a change in her life as a people pleaser. She had worked hard to earn or buy approval from a particular person who, thinking that it was Eileen who had failed to deliver some important papers to court, turned on her and verbally whipped her in front of the entire office. Eileen stood quietly, taking her undeserved punishment and trying not to crumble in front of her peers. When it was over,

Eileen sat down at her desk and fought back the tears—
tears of hurt, frustration, embarrassment, and
self-disgust. She hated herself at that moment because
she hadn't stood up for herself, hadn't defended herself, and hadn't pointed out that the attack was
undeserved because the errand had been assigned to
another person in the office.

Then and there, Eileen vowed that "never
again" would she allow herself to be in such a position.
She would learn to stand up for herself. She would not
take abuse. She was going to change. And change she
did.

If you need motivation, look at areas in your
life in which you desperately wish you were different.
Allow yourself to experience the frustration, the disgust,
the longing to be different. Capture those feelings. Remember them. When you are tempted to turn back from
your course toward freedom, pull out your feelings and
relive them. They will keep you on course.

Ask a good friend for honest feedback about
how you come across in relationships. Listen to the possibly negative information and use it as motivation to
make positive life changes.

Talk to people who have made the transition
from *You Only* or *You First* relationships to *We* relationships. Ask them to tell you their stories. Listen
carefully. Use their success to motivate you to follow in
their footsteps.

Look to the Lord for guidance, for we are
promised that if we do so, He will direct our paths *in
all of our ways* (Prov. 3:5–6).

3. Build a plan. After you have made a firm
decision to make changes, turn that decision into a
resolve. A resolve is a promise to yourself and a vow
to God that you are committed to a course of action.
Write out several resolves, starting with the words,
"I will . . ."

Look at the goals you have written. Do not expect to change overnight. You will change one step at a time, one day at a time, one experience at a time.

Think of Abraham. God called him to come away from his homeland and his people into a new land where God would make him the father of a new nation. But Abraham's journey began with one step at a time. He didn't become the father of a new nation or complete the journey overnight. It took him years to reach the place God had called him to and to leave the people God called him from (Gen. 11:27–12:9).

Keep your steps small. Don't try to reach all of your goals at once. Choose two or three to work on at a time. It takes both emotional and physical energy to make life changes. If you try to do too much, you will run out of energy and you will fail. Pace yourself.

This means that you will need to prioritize your goals and decide which ones you will work on first. Some people start working on the most important goals first, which is fine. However, there is something to be said for starting with a few of the easier goals. As you begin to see progress, your commitment to the plan will grow and your strength and courage will also increase and develop. Once you have successfully achieved five or six smaller goals, you are in a better position psychologically to tackle more difficult goals because you will know that you *can* succeed and you will be *expecting* success. Often people who start with the most difficult goals are secretly expecting failure, so they fail.

4. Understand what you can expect. There are risks as well as rewards in making life changes.

• *Discomfort.* At first you can expect to feel uncomfortable because you will be behaving in new ways. You will be trying new skills, and they will feel awkward. Remember the first time you had a skiing, bowling, or golf lesson? For years you walked, threw, and hit a certain way. Suddenly you were being told to assume different positions and make different moves. You probably felt awkward and out of place. But with repeated practice, you became more comfortable and graceful. The same is true when beginning to use new skills in dealing with people in relationships.

• *Support or resistance.* Other people will respond to you differently. Some of your supportive friends will cheer you on, encourage, and affirm you, even when your awkwardness shows. Some of your "friends" will not want you to change. They like you just as you are, spending your energies trying to please them.

• *Failure.* There will be times along the way when you will fail. You may abandon the new behavior and slip back into your old, comfortable people-pleasing rut. You may come on too strong, or even be rude because you are exploring unknown territory and may go past assertive behavior to aggressive behavior. When this happens, you will simply need to make adjustments in your behaviors, not abandon the plan altogether.

After each time you fail to fully implement the new behaviors, evaluate your performance (did you avoid eye contact, were you nervous, did you laugh inappropriately, were you vague in what you said, did you give long-winded explanations for your choices, were you hesitant, whining, pleading, or sarcastic, or was your tone of voice too loud or too soft?). Decide what you want to change the next time you encounter a similar situation.

Your failures will only be situational; they will be short-term. Soon they will decrease in frequency. Most of them will go away as you continue practicing the new behaviors.

• *Success.* You can also expect success, for you will succeed, even in the very beginning. You will make choices which are right for you. You will choose to please God rather than seek the approval of others. You will made better decisions. After each time you succeed, evaluate your performance. Identify what you did right (eye contact, listening quietly, speaking firmly but kindly, adopting a relaxed posture, expressing your thoughts precisely, using "I" statements, avoiding sarcasm, not whining or pleading, avoiding self-justification, and not backing down in spite of the response of the other person).

Celebrate these times. Plan for more of these to occur. When you succeed, share your progress with a trusted friend. Get affirmation for what you have achieved. Talk through the experience. Discuss what you did right and why and how it felt. Recapture the good feelings to use to motivate yourself for additional changes.

If you continue working according to your plan, your long-term success will be ensured. You will become more comfortable with the new skills, and you will have made positive life changes. You will be set free. You will want to continue to choose to live free and to not be entangled again in the bondage of being a people pleaser (see Gal. 5:1).

5. *Become disciplined.* It is not enough to get affirmation and then hope for continued success. You need to become disciplined in the implementation of your plan. Author, speaker, and entrepreneur Jim Rohn says, "Affirmation without discipline is the beginning of delusion; but affirmation with discipline can have staggering results."

If you are to be successful, you will need to practice daily. You can't expect to develop skills with a hit-and-miss approach. If you only play golf once every two years, you probably have not become a good golfer. One becomes skillful with frequent practice. You can become a better golfer by taking lessons, playing three times a week, and constantly evaluating your performance and making corrections which improve your play. The same is true in all areas of your life.

Don't wait for circumstances to thrust upon you opportunities to change. Practice by role-playing with a trusted friend. At the end of chapters 4–10 you found suggested situations you might use to practice the skills discussed in those chapters. Use these as a basis for developing discipline. Write additional situations and practice those. Seek out opportunities every day in which you can practice your new skills. You will be surprised at how many you will find.

Personal development and change is more than a philosophy, and success takes more than enthusiasm and self motivation—it requires discipline.

You are a steward of your personhood. It has been given you by God, and you need to be a faithful steward. Don't give away your life (1 Cor. 4:2). Arm yourself with spiritual armor and stand firm against any attacks on your resolve (Eph. 6:12–18).

6. Share what you learn. Once you have begun to see success in your own life, you will want to be open about the changes you are making because you may be able to assist others who also need to change.

HELP OTHERS CHANGE

As you begin to change, some people will come to you and ask you what is happening. Some of these people will want to know because they want to change also. As you become empowered in your own life by taking charge and setting goals with God's priorities for you in mind, you become available to be a mentor to others.

You don't become a mentor by taking out an advertisement in the newspaper or by forcing your assistance upon others. You can't mentor everyone who needs help. But if you are available and willing to share what you have learned and your successes and setbacks, you can begin to help others. A mentor must be gentle and patient, understanding that other people will pick and choose what to accept from what is shared. Not everything which was helpful or essential for you will be considered important by others.

What exactly does a mentor do?

1. A mentor observes. One of the women I admire, Rhoda, is a mentor at work for women who want to climb the corporate ladder. She has been successful and has become a senior vice president of her company, an unusual job for a woman. When young women come to her for advice, she tells them to set an appointment in about thirty days. In the interim, she reviews the records on that employee and goes out of her way to observe unobtrusively that employee on the job. She notices interactions, responses, and work habits. When they meet at the scheduled time, Rhoda is prepared with some specific observations about how that employee might make changes which would assist in her advancement. A mentor is not a spy, but an observer.

2. A mentor listens. The next thing Rhoda does is ask the young woman to tell about herself, her work experiences, and her goals. Rhoda listens carefully, noting patterns in relationships and examples of beliefs which might be nonproductive for one who wants to advance within the company.

3. A mentor provides information. Rhoda then shares information about the best ways to advance within the company, which career ladders are the quickest, and what behaviors will get the employee positive notice. She provides information and resources, and offers to be available for counsel in the future. This does not mean that all of the young women who come to Rhoda have unlimited access to her time, but as she works with a selected few at a time, they each get personal attention. She will meet for lunch once a month with each young woman.

4. A mentor models. A mentor is only respected when living what he or she is teaching. A janitor might have worked for the company for twenty years and have carefully observed how the company works. The janitor might be able to tell a young woman how to get ahead in the company, but the best advice, the most valued advice has to come from someone who has walked the journey for themselves.

5. A mentor empowers. A good mentor provides only as much assistance as is needed to direct the person to the proper resources and channels, but not so much that he or she is doing the work for the protégé. There is a need for encouragement, affirmation, attention, and even approval from the mentor, but the work must be done by the person wanting to fulfill a dream.

6. A mentor sets free. The goal of a mentor is to have the protégé move on, let go of the "training wheels," succeed, and even someday become a mentor to someone else. Often a protégé will surpass the mentor in some ways, becoming more of a success than the mentor has been in one or more areas.

There are many examples of mentoring in the Bible. Elijah passed on a double measure of his spirit along with his mantle to his protégé, Elisha. (2 Kings 2:1–15). Barnabas mentored John Mark; Moses mentored Joshua; Jesus mentored His disciples; and Paul said to the believers, "Be ye followers of me, even as I also am of Christ" (1 Cor. 11:1).

Through mentoring, you have a chance to give back what you have received. Even if no one else has given to you, God has, through the power of the Holy Spirit. All of the gifts in the New Testament were given to give away. We receive salvation and are told to share our faith (Matt. 28:19–20). We have spiritual gifts to use for the edification of the body (Eph. 4:12). We receive comfort to give that same comfort to others (2 Cor. 1:3–5).

The same is true with our success and our learning. We need to pass it on. For as we help others, we ourselves continue to learn, to grow, and to become better. Also, the kingdom is enhanced as we put back into it what we have gained.

GOD'S PERSON

Marie tells her story and smiles. She says she is a recovering people pleaser. "Now," she says happily, "I am God's person."

That's a goal we could all adopt. Joshua told the Israelites that they had to choose which gods they were going to serve. They couldn't continue to claim to serve the one God, Jehovah, and still worship other pagan gods (Josh. 24:15). Jesus repeated the warning in Matt. 6:24. He said that we can't serve two masters— we cannot be faithful to God and mammon. We have to choose. That tells me that we can't serve God by making the opinion and approval of others a "god" in our lives. We have to choose—are we going to be people pleasers or God pleasers?

Somewhere along the way, some of us have developed a belief that if we choose to live God's way we will be miserable and unhappy. Who said that was true? Whoever it was couldn't have been more wrong. Trying to please *people* is a miserable lifestyle. Choosing to be God's person brings us a much more exciting life.

Jesus said that one of the reasons He came to earth was to bring us the abundant life, that we could have His joy, and that our joy would be full (John 10:10, 15:11).

When Esther was asked to go to the king and request that the Jewish nation be saved, she was told that perhaps this opportunity was the very reason she had been placed by God in the palace (Esther 4:14).

The same may be true for you where you are right now. The opportunity of becoming God's person is the reason you were born (Rom. 8:29). When you are living the way God would have you live, you don't have to wonder if you are being a doormat, a passive person, an aggressive person, or an assertive person. You are developing proper attitudes and good habits. You are practicing a loving lifestyle, confident that you are valued and worthy as a child of the living God. You are seeking His will for your life and choosing to please God rather than men. You are being healed from the bondage of people pleasing. And you will experience incredible joy. You will be like the healed man who jumped for joy and went about praising God for his new life (Acts 3:2–11).

Become the person God created you to be. Explore all of your spiritual gifts and natural abilities. Discover your potential. Develop your personal power in Christ as you become strong, caringly assertive, independent, and accountable.

Along your journey, be open to people God will bring into your life to challenge and confront you about your life choices. Remember my friend, Steve, who helped me begin my journey by confronting me and urging me to take a hard look at my life? He was one of those "signpost" people who made a significant contribution to my life because I listened.

In the years since I met Steve at a crossroads in my life, I have often wished I knew where to reach him to tell him of a particularly significant success I've had. I know that he would have been pleased with some of the choices I've made and of the person I've become because I listened to him and acted upon his advice.

But Steve would probably be disappointed if I went to some heroic measures to find and thank him. I realized that he wanted me to change not to please him, but because it was right for me. I needed to make the changes in order to become God's person. And so I haven't tried to find Steve.

In all honesty, I didn't make the changes to please Steve. I made them because I wanted my life to be the abundant life Jesus promised I could have. I wanted to glorify God with my life. And God is faithful. I thank Him for the ever-increasing joy and freedom I am experiencing in my journey from pleasing others to pleasing Him, experiencing His best for me in my life.

Thank you, God, for what you are doing in my life.

And, Steve, wherever you are, thank you, too.